Shadow Entities

Sleep Paralysis and Beyond

Gemma Jade

BEYOND THE FRAY

Publishing

ISBN 13: 978-1-954528-54-3

Cover design: Disgruntled Dystopian Publications

Beyond The Fray Publishing, a division of Beyond The Fray, LLC, San
Diego, CA
www.beyondthefraypublishing.com

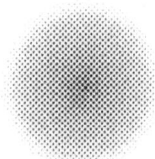

BEYOND THE FRAY

Publishing

Dedication

To my mother, Carol Barbarulo. Thank you for always supporting me and for encouraging my interest in the paranormal from a very young age. Also, for never dismissing my abilities or making me feel weird about them. Love you mom! I hope this helps you too!

Contents

Introduction

In my field of work, I come across a lot of strange and bizarre information, and normally I am all too pleased to share it with the public who take the time to watch my channel and read my books. A lot of it is anecdotal, and I use it to start conversations in the streams when I feel there is a lull. This, however, is not one of those topics. Though I am sure you will find it quite interesting, it's a bit terrifying to most people to just randomly insert into a conversation. The fact that it is one million percent true is also something most people will have a hard time wrapping their heads around. I am here now to inform you all of what is happening all around us and to call your attention to it all, as I know most of us, even in this community, aren't even aware of it all. That's what makes this even scarier to me.

The fact that, with all of the abilities floating around throughout this community and just in general, most human beings have no idea that any of this is happening. Okay, so in truth a lot of us may have a clue, but do we really know the extent as to which we are another, or several others for that matter, creatures' food? I mean, no wonder there is such rampant sickness and lethargy, depression and even addiction. This is by no means or in any way, shape, or form saying that mental illness doesn't exist and that it's always the case that some creature is feeding off the person's energy and spirit, but I will say this—I am fairly certain and, in fact, mostly sure that this is the cause of most of the human suffering in those specific ways almost all of the time. Whatever it causes, as each person subjected to this type of vampiric feeding is different, it's never a good thing, and I truly hope that by bringing this to you all now, it will help you not only to understand that it's really happening but how it happens and also, maybe, how to at least stand a fighting chance at preventing it.

We all should know by now that this world is not everything it appears to be. We all wake in the morning and go about our daily lives, and no matter what that may look like for you—the one constant, whether you're aware of it or not—is the fact that in the darkness of the places we cannot see—and I don't mean that there's no light and it's dark—although I'm sure it's happening then too, but in broad daylight and all over the world—there is something terribly dark and sinister taking place that most people, even sensitives and those with certain abilities—just aren't aware of. Sure, as I already stated earlier, most people can sense there's SOMETHING happening and that it's negative, but only some of us can actually SEE it. More and more people are waking up every single day and realizing they have certain abilities in them that they never noticed before. So, with more and more people waking up, recognizing and possibly even learning how to use their own abilities for the greater good of the collective, there is still a very large fraction of humanity that haven't the slightest clue and know nothing of even the concept that we are literally food. No idea about the things that come in and out of our dimension that most of us can't even see and some of us can't even sense, who energetically take from us. This has all been going on since the dawn of time, and we are just now, as a collective, coming to even have an inkling of it. It's that powerful.

Whether or not being more aware is going to do any good and make any real sort of difference is solely based on how much of this, if any, you're willing to believe. It's not a joke and it's not going away. In fact, it all seems to be getting worse and happening so much more nowadays than ever before. Maybe by the end of this we will have some kind of answer to or reasoning for that. It used to be that almost exclusively people with "abilities" were subject to these types of things but not anymore. There is an absolutely ghastly number of paranormal and otherworldly entities, energies and creatures that torture us, physically, mentally, emotionally, spiritually and psychically and also that utterly terrify us. It's nothing new, and they've been doing it for millennia. They are parasitic in nature, and it is definitely not a symbiotic relationship I am talking about here. These things are monstrous. They're leeches who not only feed on us but suck us almost dry in all of the above-mentioned ways. These creatures feed on our sexual energy, our often very high states of emotion and even our life force! They roam around, most of them in the form of energy, and just lurk and wait for the right moment, usually while we are operating at our lowest frequency but sometimes at our highest too (think sexual here), and then they pounce on us and begin to feed almost until we are completely drained. Almost. This is definitely not a good situation, as these things, individually and separately, hate and despise us, yet they need us in order to survive, and this is, at least according to popular opinion on the subject, the reason they don't just kill us off and take the planet for themselves. I'm positive they wish to do just that but can't because without us, they would starve to death.

There is extensive data that proves that the soul or the human life force—however you wanna put it and whatever name you give it doesn't really matter, as it's all the same thing—is something that every single one of these entities undoubtedly needs to survive. Our soul, our essence, our energy, our very BEING! Even scarier is that they are so multifaceted that between them they can take on almost any shape, size and image that they choose to at any given time.

Have you ever had one of those nightmares that was so incredibly intense you wake up not only scared out of your damn mind but also in a state of panic and with some sort of deep sense that perhaps it wasn't a nightmare at all but had actually happened? Even when it's something you wake up like this to but can't even remember what it is? That's because most of the time, in this scenario at least, it DID happen, it just happened when you were sleeping and at your most vulnerable. You're mentally, emotionally, physically, psychically and even spiritually drained. You're exhausted and feel as though you haven't slept in days despite having just woken up—even from a solid eight hours. Your entire day is off because you're unusually lethargic and perhaps you don't even feel like doing anything you have to do that day at all. It sounds all too familiar, doesn't it? Are you finding this happening more and more lately? In more recent years?

Let me set a scene here for you to imagine—you're up and panicked, terrified and confused and know somewhere deep down that what just happened in your worst nightmare really happened... somehow. Do you chalk it up to you being paranoid or foolish? Then please understand that that is exactly what these things bet on. They think we are stupid and simply food for them and nothing else, and they can almost guarantee that most of us won't even give it a second thought once we are out of bed and on with our day. Most of us are over it by the time we are consuming our morning coffee or green tea blends.

I know it sounds odd, but even dreams aren't always dreams. With the dark must come the light, and with the good must come the bad, right? I wonder why it's so easy for us to believe a dream, perhaps about a deceased loved one coming to give us a message, could have been a real message and a real visitation, but we draw a hard line at believing the same for nightmares. This is, of course, where the shadow people and sleep paralysis come into play. Those incessantly annoying and very creepy entities who usually manifest between the hours of midnight and 4 a.m. Essentially, when it's dark outside.

I'm sure whether you've ever personally encountered them or not, every single one of you just got an image of one type of shadow entity or another in your head that you saw or heard about somewhere you can't quite place. Yes, you can see them during the day as well, and a lot of people, again more so in recent years, do see them in the day and night and inside as well as outside. For the most part and throughout history though, the darkest hours for us are their most chosen time to appear and do their damage... Or depending on the type, do... whatever it is that they do. These things, at least the hostile ones, which I call the sleep paralysis demons, literally paralyze us and vampirically feed off of our energy and essence. They feed off of our fear and our life force, just as the vampires like the ones in the Ann Rice novels hold people down and feed off of their blood.

There's been cases where the elusive and mythical vampire of ancient legend and lore has obtained for themselves what they call donors. Donors are humans who are said to voluntarily give their blood to the vampires so they can feed, and it's almost unheard of for the creature to drain the donor. What good would that do? That's exactly what I liken to the shadow people and the so-called sleep paralysis they put us into. Who knows, and some would say it's a fact, while I am mainly just considering it, it makes sense that perhaps the bloodsucking vampires we know and have grown to love thanks to modern-day fiction got their start in this world thanks to the nameless, hardly seen and therefore unknown shadows that feed on our energy in the night. Is it possible that someone knew exactly what was going on and just decided to put a face to it and change a few of the details?

If you want to know or are expecting to learn here exactly what the shadow people or shadow entities are, then you are out of luck. The topic simply of what they are is subject to a lot of drama and so much debate. Everyone has their opinions as to what these multidimensional beings are and what they want, where they come from and how long they've been here. Every single thing about them is technically unknown. Even those of us who may think we know really can't back it up with facts and evidence. There is data, but even that varies depending on who you speak to and who collected it. Do they come from the fourth dimension? Are they like us only without light and therefore seek us out to restore their own light? Is our light a part of the essence they seem so desperate to steal from us in the middle of the night while we are asleep and most vulnerable? All really great and reasonable questions. All without final answers.

There are a few people who are considered to be a bit more knowledgeable than the rest of us though, those who have written a book or two, but again it's all just based on either secondhand accounts, speculation and/or personal experiences. Regardless of any of this and what you believe, the bottom line is that for many entities, energies and even some extraterrestrials, we ARE their food. The question I am most asked by clients and even random people who approach me is, "Is there anything we can DO about any of this?" The answer to that is a resounding YES! That's exactly what I want to delve deep into in this book. Come and take a walk with me through the terrifying unknown and get to know the creatures that so often make us their prey and we don't even know it. The only time we recognize them is when they appear, cloaked in the darkness of night, in the middle of what we are calling "sleep paralysis" episodes. It's not all that simple though... It's really not.

Chapter 1

In the Darkness of the Night

It's almost become common for me to ask myself the question of whether or not my lifelong and seemingly irrational fear of the dark is my being afraid of the actual darkness itself or possibly my fearing what's inside it. As I sit and ponder this question for the millionth time, I have to wonder, if it's the latter, then what exactly do I think is in there? As I lay in bed at night with all the lights off in the complete silence and pitch black of my bedroom, what is it that is causing an almost paralyzing terror inside me and all throughout my body? While everyone's eyes adjust to the blackness eventually, it's never to the point where we can actually see as good as when there's light. Am I taking random and inanimate objects and turning them into the horrific and terrifying things I think I am seeing, or are those things actually there with me? Lurking in some hidden corner of the room, thinking it's either unseen or not sensed. Could that be it? Could it be there is an inner knowing in me and everyone else who has ever experienced something like this? Something that's hidden inside all of us somewhere and totally primal? Is it an intuition of sorts that tells us when something just isn't right or is flat-out wrong?

More and more lately I am hearing about people being attacked by something that is sometimes referred to as a shadow entity or being. Some of us refer to them as shadow people because a lot of the time they take the shape of a man, a humanoid and bipedal blackness. There are many different types of shadow entities being reported as well, and the phenomenon definitely seems to be on the rise in the last ten years or so. I have found that giving them titles makes it easier to discuss them with my clients or others who come to me with their experiences. While these are by no means the only types of shadow entities to ever have been encountered, in this book I will discuss, at length, the ones I have most come across. There are the benign entities, the lurkers, the cowboys, the hat men, the observers, the females, the travelers, the attackers, the pets— sometimes called ferals—the tricksters, the extraterrestrials, the sleep paralysis demons, who we will learn are the worst of their kind and who are on a fiendish mission like no other entity I have ever come across. That is, aside from the final type of shadow being on our list, the Djinn. In a league all their own, the Djinn could very well be the most feared and the most dangerous type of shadow entity out there.

They are said to be capable of not only causing physical harm to human beings but also death. On top of these several types of humanoid entities, there is a subgroup, if you will, and those are the creepers, the black masses and the black mists.

There are so many encounters, yet there is so little known about the entities in general, those covered by the umbrella title of "shadow people," and still less about the entities individually. I've found that they are a humanoid shape that is ALMOST always male in appearance. Apart from the travelers, they seem to be aware of us and oftentimes will react to our reactions to them. They are uncommonly tall, often reported as being between six and seven feet tall or possibly taller. They appear to have a certain depth to them. They are not easily mistaken for a simple and regular shadow, as one may think, because they are not flat to the wall and have obvious density to them. They are reported as wearing or being wrapped in a large, old-fashioned coat or cloak, oftentimes with a hood up over their heads. For the most part they have no visible features at all except for, every once in a while, glowing eyes of various colors. The most commonly reported color the eyes are said to glow is red. They have absolutely no regard for physical objects such as pieces of furniture or even walls and walk right through them as if they aren't there at all. The fact of the matter is that despite so many commonalities across thousands upon thousands of encounter stories, there is just no way to nail down these entities unless we break them up as though each category I present to you were a different species altogether—while also keeping in mind that they very well could be just that. However, we must also be mindful that it's just as possible that they are one and the same after all.

These are things that lurk not only in the pitch blackness of our bedrooms at night but also that lurk in the deepest, darkest recesses of our own minds. Could there be instances where a person is having a bad dream or some sort of visual hallucination? Sure! That's another reason we must take any information we glean and every encounter we come across at face value. We must decide what it means and what it's worth, if anything on either count, and what exactly that is. Let's face it, if it's the darkness itself we fear, then a night-light is probably the best investment we can make for ourselves; however, if it is the shadows that creep in the dark, especially when dealing with a very scared or simply overactive imagination, maybe a night-light isn't the best idea.

Then there's the scientific explanation for a lot of things that go bump in the night: pareidolia. Pareidolia is often defined as "the tendency for incorrect perception of a stimulus as an object, pattern or meaning known to the observer, such as seeing shapes in clouds, seeing faces in inanimate objects or abstract patterns, or hearing hidden messages in music." Have you ever seen faces in the smoke from a cigarette or cigar or a hidden image in the clouds? In my opinion this is just another of science's many convenient explanations for paranormal happenings. Yes, of course there are times when a person is merely making one thing out to be another thing, but honestly, at least from the people I've spoken to while writing this book and otherwise and from my own personal experiences, more often than not, there is something there. It's simply about finding the meaning in it. For example, there have been times when I've looked up at the clouds and saw an angel-shaped one and the person next to me or people with me saw the exact same thing. Some might say I am reaching here and that maybe the cloud just looked like an angel? Sure, I guess. I, however, like to look for the meaning in all of it. Why an angel just then, at that time in my/our lives? Just something to think about as we move forward here. Could it just be that we seek to create meaning when and where there is none?

This is very interesting for me right now because of the extent to which I had to study sleep paralysis in order to write this book. I won't be discussing it too much here because I really want to focus on the paranormal side of things because I personally believe only about two percent of sleep paralysis is something to do with the brain and the other ninety-eight percent really does have to do with the supernatural and otherworldly. It's important to note that pareidolia is about much more than seeing faces and shapes in the inanimate and seemingly random objects we come across on a daily basis. It also means that the experiencer is trying to make something more meaningful than it really is. I bring this up because of all the times I saw a hat on the coat rack when I would wake from a restless sleep on the couch in my completely darkened living room and was too scared to get up and wander into my bedroom because I was convinced this thing had actually taken on a life of its own. In fact, I posit to you now that perhaps some entities, especially shadow beings, know all about a lot of our scientific terms for things and use them to their own advantage. What if a shadow entity knows you will automatically assume the hat on top of the coat rack is just that and decides that's where it's going to take up residence while haunting you in the middle of the night when you wake from that restless sleep? Again, it's just as possible as anything else we will be discussing here.

I read an article from PsychCentral online that said, "Not everything in this world has meaning. We need to learn to distinguish when we're uncovering meaning from when we're constructing it." Very interesting indeed and something to ruminate on as we move forward here to the basics of the shadow entity phenomenon, and perhaps, by the end of this book, we could get just a little bit closer to finding out what it all means, if anything at all. I would be doing you a great disservice if I didn't remind you that it all works both ways. Pareidolia is making something out to be more than it is. It's making something out to be paranormal or otherworldly when really, it's just their eyes or minds playing tricks on them. There are many occasions, though, where people have come to me completely dismissing a very real and extremely dangerous situation involving a paranormal entity, such as but not limited to a shadow person encounter, and had completely and totally convinced themselves that they were just dreaming.

Lucid dreaming is being aware while dreaming that you are, in fact, dreaming. Many people tell themselves these encounters are just nightmares. Here is an encounter that's recently come to me that illustrates this point perfectly. It's from someone who would like to remain completely anonymous. This person chalked their very real and very terrifying experience up to, "just a really scary lucid dream." This person reported that, in the middle of the day, they decided to lie down and take a nap. Once they lay there with their eyes slowly shutting, they felt a strange fogginess in their head but decided they were merely sleep deprived from working ten straight double shifts. It was their first day off in fourteen days, and they were on the brink of exhaustion. They opened their eyes and entered into this half-dream state and suddenly heard the voice of a character from one of their favorite shows. It seemed as though it were coming from a television that sounded as though it were about two feet from the bed they were lying on. However, there was no TV in that room at all, and therefore this explanation made even less sense. This only left that someone was imitating the voice of that cartoon character and that whatever or whoever it was was right there in the room with them.

Suddenly, just as suddenly as the haziness of the mind had hit, there was a very loud, audible chorus of whooshing, ringing and popping noises in the person's ears. They couldn't tell though if the cacophony was all in their heads or actually happening, like the voice of the character they had heard only seconds ago. Our witness tried to get up despite knowing they would most likely be very dizzy and confused, as now they were afraid, they were having some sort of medical emergency, perhaps from overworking themselves. However, they quickly found that, aside from being able to move their eyeballs from side to side and blink, they were completely and totally paralyzed.

There was a window to the left side of the bed they were now incapacitated on, and they heard a very loud and sudden knocking on it. Looking with just the turn of their eyeballs, they were able to see, albeit quite unclearly, a figure. It was dark and featureless. Within the literal blink of an eye, there was a second figure, the same as the first, who was still outside the window and knocking even louder now, who was standing directly over our witness to the left side. They could see both figures now, and they were totally identical. The fear was almost too much to bear, but our witness still couldn't move, though movement in the head was coming back now. The shadow person next to the bed started to telepathically speak, "I would be afraid too. This is the stuff nightmares are made from."

Then a very dark and somewhat maniacal cackle filled the room as our witness was no longer paralyzed and jumped from their bed. There was no more fogginess and haze. There was no more noise at all in the now empty room. Our witness insists to me that they can't handle even considering the concept that this might have been much more than a lucid or very vivid dream. I, on the other hand, have a hard time believing it was anything other than a very bizarre and very terrifying, real encounter with something unknown and dark. There were no other visits to this person before or since, and they have since stopped talking about it in the hopes of being able to finally stop thinking about it.

What do you all think out there? Is this the case of a person pretending something paranormal was something altogether different, like a dream? I guess we will all base our decisions on our own knowledge and life experience. I know that I don't believe in coincidence and would rather be and think more safely than sorry. Ignoring these things never makes them go away, and I don't believe for a second our witness here has seen or heard the last of these two entities.

Chapter 2
The Basics

The term "shadow people" was allegedly first used and therefore said to have been coined by Heidi Hollis, an author who has written several books on the fast-growing phenomenon. According to Heidi, "Shadow people have been around since the beginning of time and are a dark influence upon society." There is a major force here that we are going to discuss at length in this book known as the Djinn and how they appear much of the time as simple shadow entities. However, I believe the Djinn shadow people are far more than what meets the eye, as are the "regular" ones, but we will get to all of that soon.

Throughout history there have been thousands of narrations in ancient and religious texts, fairy tales, folklore and simple, firsthand accounts of humanlike, shadowy figures. They seem to be neither entirely physical nor entirely spiritual but sort of come out of the ether every now and again to carry out whatever its intended purpose is at that particular time. Ancient

Europeans believed that these shadow entities desired blood and couldn't be reborn without it. The possible reason for these entities trying to be reborn is that they would like to possess the human body because theirs is without light. In Greece, people believed that if a person went to a specific temple—the temple of Zeus Lycaeus, they would lose their shadows. They believed Lycaeus to be responsible for the creation of the first werewolves. This is the most likely reason behind the legends of entities such as vampires, werewolves and witches, being cursed, lacking a shadow or reflection.

In medieval times if you were accusing someone of being a witch or some other sort of unholy creature of the night whose soul was sold or otherwise belonging to Satan, you had to prove your claim by showing that the person was lacking a shadow and/or reflection.

Plutarch was a Greek Middle Platonist philosopher, biographer, essayist, and priest at the Temple of Apollo. He seemingly had a whole other theory about why a human being would be lacking a shadow and said, "At the end of the world, the blessed ones would be happy forever. In a state neither needing food nor casting a shadow."

Reports of encounters with them are found throughout every single culture and in every nation around the world. Because they appear in the peripheral vision much of the time, it's nearly impossible for those people to even be able to articulate what it was they saw, aside from the fact that it had a humanlike form and was bipedal. Except, of course, for the occasional glowing eyes, which were for centuries being reported only as red but now are being reported as yellow and even green as well. In more recent years more and more people have been reporting being able to see the full form of the figure and also to be able to see them head on. It all depends on your specific experience. Each one being just as unique as these entities themselves are.

While skeptics will try to chalk shadow people encounters up to lack of sleep and delirium or other things to that effect, I myself beg to differ, as there is simply too much information out there that says otherwise. After all, we are brought together in this community by our experiences. Even if I cannot convince you totally that these beings are in fact real and not just a figment of a sleep-deprived, possibly drug-addled mind, I hope you will, by the end of this book, be much more educated and come out of all of it with a more open mind. The paranormal world is tricky to present because there is no clear and convincing evidence available when presenting the information.

Keeping in mind that our peripheral vision was literally designed so we could detect motion and movement that is out of our direct line of sight, we know that there are times, many times, where it IS simply playing tricks on us and all in our minds. But so many people, thousands or more, across the world and since the beginning of time, all playing the same tricks all of the time? Well to me, that's simply more fantastical and unbelievable than the subject of the shadow entities itself.

While many people who have had encounters with shadow people have done so during what we now have started calling "sleep paralysis" episodes, these are just a small number of reported encounters or attacks of and from these things. They are annoyingly blurry and shockingly fast and therefore one of the most frustrating paranormal entities I've ever had the extreme displeasure of encountering because I can never really get a good look at them when I see them in my peripheral vision as I'm going about my day to day. I've seen shadow people, and I know I'm not alone here, in broad daylight as well as in the darkness of the middle of the night. I've encountered them just seeming to stand and stare at me, knowing I was looking right at it but not seeming to care in the least. I've been literally attacked by them dozens upon dozens of times throughout my life, during sleep paralysis episodes and while definitely wide awake.

These specific entities seem to really get around, and the term "shadow person" is basically just lumping together all entities that are pitch black and seemingly made of nothing, of shadow, I guess. But that's so wrong. I look at shadow people specifically as any of the humanoid, human-shaped black and dark entities that haunt my sleep at night and my daily boring life as well and also the masses and mists I previously mentioned. Whether or not they actually

DO anything or not, they're still at most terrifying and at the very least quite eerie to encounter. They seem to be able to show themselves anywhere and everywhere at any time of the day or night too. They seem to have no limit as far as when they can appear or disappear either. How many times can we see something darting around super-fast out of the corners of our eyes and dismiss it as just our imagination? I find that most people do just this when having an encounter with any kind of supernatural or paranormal being. They do everything they possibly can to convince themselves that they aren't seeing what they are seeing. That they aren't experiencing and feeling exactly what they are. I believe that this is what so many supernatural entities and negative energies, including the shadow people, depend on. They can assume for almost certain that we are going to try to explain them away and therefore leave them free to roam and stalk and basically slowly take over our homes, our thoughts and even our dreams at night.

These are the types of cases that I am always looking to report on whether in my books, my YouTube videos or even just generally because science is working hard to explain away the very real phenomenon of attacks during sleep paralysis as a trick of the brain, and in some cases that could very well be what's happening, but in thousands of cases across the world over? I'm not buying it. So, these cases where the person is awake and thinking very coherently are the ones I really like to try to focus on when presenting my research. I believe that shadow people are actually an intelligent life form despite their lack of vocabulary. I've never heard of an actual shadow entity ever speaking to anyone. Maybe there have been a few cases where they telepathically said something, but in those cases I'm wary. Maybe that wasn't a simple shadow being, then.

In 2010, a woman from Tennessee in the United States claims to have had what I think is one of the most random and bizarre shadow person encounters I've yet to come across. Not the most terrifying, mind you, but just so... well, random, as I said. She claims that after dropping her daughter off at the school bus stop, she decided to go out on her deck and enjoy the fresh air and bright sunshine with a cup of coffee. She was by herself out there and says the deck is a little more than twelve feet off the ground and it wraps around the house. She was standing on the part that faces the back of her house, into her backyard.

As she was standing out there enjoying her coffee and the warm spring air at a little before seven in the morning, she turned her head and noticed an extremely dark black, human-shaped figure standing on one of the other sides of her deck. It was also facing the backyard and leaning on the rails. It had no facial features at all and definitely wasn't a human being but a Being, and a very solid, very dark one. She claimed that as she stood there staring, I'm sure with her mouth hanging wide open and speechless, this thing turned and looked at her and, as it seemed to notice her, started moving backwards. Not walking backwards but floating. She described its movements as "catlike," which I took to mean as it was a bit more graceful looking than a regular human being, as this is how these creatures and many others in the paranormal community seem to move, with a kind of graceful fluidity to their motion that couldn't ever even remotely be mistaken for human. She also likened it to when a cat stalks its prey, that sort of prowling-type motion. A creeping, if you will, only backwards.

The woman said as the thing moved slowly away from her, it dragged its "hand" across the wood of the deck. Take that into consideration for a moment if you will: the deck is twelve feet tall or more, and this thing is dragging its hand against the very top of it! She claims she got a very peaceful and warm feeling at watching it slowly float backwards. The story doesn't go on to say how the thing left her view, only saying that the black "hands" were the last she saw of the being before it was gone. Did it float away? Did it disappear slowly or vanish in a blink? Unfortunately, these details weren't recounted.

She goes on to say that the entity didn't speak to her or say anything. I believe it actually did though, only it did so telepathically. While there were no words spoken, she says she somehow got the impression of, "I'm not going to hurt you today, but I could if I wanted to." Well, if that isn't telepathic communication, I'm not sure what is! Give her a break, though, as most people who see these entities become engulfed in the fear and feelings of the moment and don't even realize what they're seeing half the time, let alone that the thing is actually communicating something to them. I'm not sure what's worse, the fact that it let her know it could hurt her but had chosen not to, or having no communication with the thing at all. She says she never went out onto her back deck again after that day. Who could blame her? Though if I really were to think about it, I think this was more intriguing than scary, and me being me, I would probably not be able to leave well enough alone and would go back out, day after day, looking for more.

This encounter is rare for a number of reasons. The first being it was an outside encounter and also that it happened in broad daylight. Also, whether she believes it communicated or not, as I said, in my opinion it definitely did. I chose this particular encounter to start off with because it contains so many of the variables we hardly ever see such as what I've already stated above. This is considered to be a "basic" encounter because it was there, she saw it, and it left. Done deal.

Chapter 3
The Benign

Benign shadow entities are categorized as such because they never hurt or harm the witness and usually leave or disappear when spotted. While some of the other types of shadow entities we will discuss here could have what could technically be considered benign encounters, the entities themselves are questionable and usually have other characteristics that make them more suitable for another category. For example, a person may have an encounter with a hat man entity, and it may be considered a benign encounter, but that doesn't mean the hat man is benign, and in fact, he is the farthest thing from it.

With the benign entities there is never a feeling of dread or fear instilled in the witness. This isn't to say that someone who sees one of these entities isn't scared out of their wits at the experience, but there is more of an elemental fear that's felt on a more primal level when experiencing or witnessing some of the scarier, more evil types of these beings. These figures do not usually purposely interact with human beings, and in fact, they normally don't even seem to perceive the presence of the human, and vice versa, until some outside event should happen to trigger the sighting. An event such as turning to look at exactly the right moment and just happening to catch a glimpse of the figure coming, going or even standing still in one part of the room or another. It's important to understand here that the benign shadow entities are easily able to be categorized as any of the other types as well. It all depends on the individual experience.

I've recently come across some speculation that claims these particular entities are deceased loved ones just visiting and looming around a person or place they loved very much in life. However, I think this is a very dangerous assumption to make, and with my extensive knowledge of the afterlife and how Spirit presents itself, I find it very hard to believe this theory and do not subscribe to it myself. Similar to the observer type of shadow people, whom we will discuss in a later chapter, though they may or may not seem to be observing you, the benign shadow people usually seem to at least be curious about something. These types of shadow entities will oftentimes, when they notice they've been spotted, cock their heads to one side similar to what a dog does when it seems to be curious about or questioning something. They are even known to sometimes approach the human, with caution of course, when they know they're being stared at.

An example that comes to mind is one day when I was folding my laundry in the bedroom of a small apartment back in 2004, and I noticed something move out of the corner of my eye. I looked, and to my surprise there was a shadow figure just standing there —in broad daylight too! It wasn't looking at me at first, I knew this because the head shape seemed to be turned, and it was looking to the right as though it had turned its head when I had opened the door to enter the room and never bothered to turn it back forward, towards where I was now standing. However, most likely upon hearing my gasp, it did turn and look directly at me. I am not the typical witness, mind you, as I have been seeing and hearing much more terrifying things than a random shadow person in the corner of my room my entire life. It didn't even invoke any sort of fear in me. I kept staring at it but also went about haphazardly folding my laundry. I was reluctant to take my eyes off it, as I wasn't as familiar with these entities at that time, and I had only heard of people being attacked by them.

It stared straight back at me, and there we were, stuck in this seemingly endless staring contest until, tentatively, it took a step forward. Just one step. Of course, I took a step backward, and I could actually feel its curiosity and hesitation. It cocked its head to the side as if to say, "may I approach?" I felt myself telepathically answering in the affirmative, so it did approach. It took two more steps towards me, cocked its head to the left again, and just as suddenly as it had been there, it was gone. It had completely blinked out of existence! Now, this is absolutely an extreme case, but I assure you it is nowhere near one of a kind. I have received at least a dozen reports of people experiencing the exact same thing. I was a bit flustered when the entity just disappeared like that, and I was suddenly left with an overwhelming sense of annoyance that there hadn't been a purpose for its appearance made known to me. A part of me felt like it wanted or needed something that I had somehow failed to understand, and therefore it gave up and left. I have absolutely no way of knowing if my feelings were right or valid, but they are what I felt at that moment.

I've had several other encounters with benign entities, and it's usually in the dead of night when I get up and go downstairs for a drink with nothing but tiny night-lights lighting my way through my hallway, down the stairs into my den, through my living room and then my dining room until, finally, I can get into the kitchen and turn the light on. It's an eerie thing to see these entities head on and know they're just there, kind of lurking around but seemingly with no real intent or purpose, at least not one I am capable of understanding.

These entities also stand out as different compared to the lurker who will try to hide when it is seen and who seem to take on unnatural shapes so as to blend in with the furniture or into a darkened corner. More often than not the benign entities will appear to be "shocked" when sighted. For instance, when a human being walks into their kitchen and sees a shadow person there in the middle of the room and it stops and turns to the human almost as though it were a child caught red-handed with its fingers in the cookie jar. I say this too because this is the exact feeling that's been recounted to me time and time again: someone feeling as though the entity were caught off guard somehow. Who can ever possibly be sure what it really was doing or intending to do when caught like that?

This brings to mind an encounter a friend of mine had back in 2010. He told me that he was sitting in his living room and heard noises like dishes were being scattered around in the kitchen next to him. He tried to ignore it but was wondering if a field mouse or some other rodent or creature had somehow gotten into his cupboards. He got up and walked slowly into his kitchen, and when he flipped on the light, there in the middle of the kitchen, right at the counter over the sink, was a tall shadow person. He said it stopped and stood stone still when it realized it had been sighted and started to slowly back up. My friend said he almost chuckled to himself because it seemed to him like the thing was trying to walk slowly enough so as to not be seen—when it was quite obviously right there in his face. The entity eventually backed up enough and went right into a side wall that led down into his basement, and he never saw it or any other entity again. He said it was almost like when he played hide-and-seek with his four-year-old grandson, and he hid in plain sight with his hands over his eyes. The mentality of "if I can't see you, you can't see me" was exactly what kept running through his mind. He didn't even think to be scared until afterwards when he thought about what he had actually witnessed. What had this entity wanted? Why was it rummaging through his kitchen? Was it looking for something? More importantly, was it somehow trying to telepathically convey to my friend that he wasn't in fact seeing what he was seeing and to somehow, albeit unsuccessfully, confuse him? Very strange indeed.

These entities also do not invoke any type of extremely negative type of emotions when they're spotted like the absolute fear and terror one feels, almost on a primal level, when confronted with most other shadow beings. Any encounter with or sighting of any type of shadow entity, including the benign ones, could indicate some sort of psychic or even spiritual attack. Maybe this is why they appear in places like our kitchens and seem to be rummaging through our cabinets. Maybe our soul is under such duress we are seeing them as some sort of harbinger of a personal spiritual warfare. I find the benign shadows very fitting for this scenario, as I can't figure out for the life of me what their purpose is if it isn't to feed off of fear. Could seeing one really be nothing more than a bad omen?

The following is a submission I found where it seems the person is dealing with a shadow creature, given the height of the thing. Everything else they say, though, is reminiscent of either a benign shadow entity or an observer. "I recently bought a 96 yr old house, I have had experiences with ghosts before but this I cannot explain. It makes me uneasy and a little scared, and I don't get scared easily. It stands outside my bedroom door, never comes in, and just stares at me! It's only about 3ft tall, it's black, like an outline of somebody, but it has bright white eyes. Where I have to turn my back to my door, but still feel it looking. What should I do and does it seem evil b/c it sure makes me feel that way."

Demons are the only entities I have ever known to just stand and lurk in bedroom doorways, and when a shadow entity is shorter than five feet tall, I often wonder if there is some sort of connection or correlation between shadow entities, even the benign ones, and demons. The end result is the same in that the human victim experiences maximum fear and panic and the entity gets its food for the night. Whenever my home or life seems to be overrun with shadows and shadow entities, like when I start seeing or sensing them a lot more often than usual, I sage my home and do a ritual cleansing and spring cleaning —regardless of what season it actually is. The fact of the matter is that no shadow person or entity is able to survive in a happy atmosphere.

The exception to this is if they're attached to someone who, aside from the attachment itself, has an otherwise pure spirit and an unusually happy and calm soul. It's an absolutely ingenious cyclical pattern where the entities are drawn to some negative energy attached to a specific person or place. Once there, they find the source or sources for all of the negativity and start showing themselves and appearing to the humans in the home or area, inducing an extreme sense of fear and terror on which the entities feed and which also helps to not only perpetuate the negative atmosphere, but it's also what probably created it and drew the entities to it in in the first place. It's a very grim and desperate supernatural cycle indeed. Most people don't know that most paranormal and supernatural entities and energies actually can't enter our homes or personal space without our permission. The fact is, though, that these entities are, if not completely evil, totally lower vibrational and at the very least unkind towards humans and love to find the loopholes in the "rules." Some might say these things already have the advantage given that most of humanity is unaware that such rules and pacts even exist in the first place and not many more than that would actually believe in all of it anyway.

One thing I learned very early on in my life adventure of being a medium is that ninety-nine percent of the time the subject will actually give the entity permission to approach or even to invade without even realizing that's what they had done. We unintentionally give these things permission to leech on and feed off of us at their wills and whims. I often wonder if, aside from the cover the darkness the night provides them, perhaps this need for permission is one of the reasons these things come to us at the hours they do. Maybe they choose while we are asleep because this is when we are at our most vulnerable and our guards are the most down.

Chapter 4
While We Sleep

Throughout history and since the beginning of time there have been reports of people feeling like they are traveling outside their bodies while they sleep. Having an out-of-body experience comes with much more than just the sensation you are outside yourself and even goes much further, with some people claiming to witness themselves asleep from a different spot in the room. With more and more people reportedly having these types of feelings and experiences, the medical community has finally taken notice. In fact, OBEs are being acknowledged and even officially declared "medical mysteries." The scientific community dedicates various studies into this particular phenomenon but has yet to come up with any sort of reasonable or rational answer for it. There have been quite a few studies done by neuroscientists in which the results were published in esteemed journals and medical digests. They concluded they could use virtual reality to manipulate patient's brains to feel as though they were having an out-of-body experience. They determined it is a physical experience and therefore happens in the brain.

What about sleep paralysis, then? Many people who haven't had this experience or who are more inclined to believe in the alleged science of all of these paranormal happenings will gladly and easily accept the notion that sleep paralysis is a medical condition that causes the mind to simply imagine all of the experiences reported during an episode. The official, scientific definition of sleep paralysis is, "is characterized by the sensation of being unable to move while awakening from sleep. Sleep paralysis is described as a transitional state that occurs when a person experiences a temporary inability to react, move, or speak while asleep, falling asleep, or on awakening from sleep." However, this explanation, regardless of how "official," mentions nothing about paranormal or supernatural experiences. What, exactly is it, though, and why does it seem to be so closely connected to encounters with shadow entities? I have no idea what the answer to these questions are, and honestly as far as I can gather, neither does the scientific community, though they do claim to have a very rational explanation for the shadow person phenomenon.

In my research I see that the official psychological name for a shadow person encounter is sleep paralysis. To me this isn't really an explanation. Calling one thing by the name of how it terrorizes you just doesn't make much sense to me. Do we interchange the words heart attack and clogged arteries? No, one is the cause of the other. Sleep paralysis seems to be what brings on the shadow people, at least in sleep paralysis cases. I have noticed though, that sleep paralysis, whether caused by shadow people or not, is what makes them so emboldened to actually approach so close and terrorize the way they do. Any other time there's no physical interaction, and normally once they get what they came for, they either vanish into thin air, through a wall or walk off/float away. Not with sleep paralysis though. With this they are so bold. They will come right up to you and get right in your face and even physically assault you. Is it just their good luck to have found you this way? Are they the cause? Or are they working in tandem with something else, whether known or unknown, to know exactly when we are in one of our most vulnerable states and then attack, like any opportunist would do?

It seems the scientific community, with all of their alleged research and data, have no idea what it actually is and seem to be taking just an educated guess at this point. What I do know though is that it was far too hard to find any scientific documents or data that mentioned, at least seriously, the otherworldly feelings (mainly terror) and supernatural encounters that seem to go hand in hand with the phenomenon. It's not all science, but it's not all paranormal either. Sleep paralysis, or as it's now more commonly being referred to, "old hag syndrome," is, in its most basic explanation, when a person who is asleep wakes in an allegedly half-dreaming state, with the mind very active and awake but with the body still under the influence of sleep chemicals that do and are still in those moments keeping us paralyzed and in a sleep state. Though we aren't. It's said to be caused by a disrupted or messed-up REM cycle. REM is the dream state of sleep, and what happens is with all of this going on, we are stuck, essentially, in a kind of state where we are lucid and awake, yet also a nightmare state. Why a nightmare and not a dream? you ask. I'm not exactly sure, but I believe that it's because we are now, due to this extreme set of circumstances, aware of what's really going on around us when we are sleeping. However, scientifically, it's said to be because we are completely helpless and unable to move.

Whatever you wanna call it, sleep paralysis or something entirely different and terrifying/paranormal, it's not rare by any means. It seems to be becoming less and less rare as the years roll by. How come as the world seems to grow more evil, at least from a spiritual standpoint, we are all experiencing more and more of these terrifying things happening in the dead of night? If it was fully scientific, then wouldn't it have been common across the board—meaning across the ages? The estimate right now is that up to 50 percent of people in the world will experience sleep paralysis at least once in their lives. The result is always absolutely traumatizing and full of horror and fear.

Here is what one person reported while having what they believed to be a sleep paralysis episode, "I have a few different 'sleep paralysis demons.' The demon ones are the usual shadowy figures standing over me or by my bedroom door. The worst one was while I was lying on my side with my back to the door and it felt like someone got into bed behind me. Under the covers and put their arm around my waist. Then it felt like they were cuddling into me and I could feel breath on my neck. It felt like they cuddled me for about half an hour. All this time I'm trying not to show that I'm panicking because it feels like I'm getting cuddled by a skeleton with claws. It was only about the second, maybe third time I'd had sleep paralysis, so I nearly had a heart attack when this thing feels like it's moving in closer to kiss me behind the ear. Worst of all it whispered 'Not yet. You're not ready yet. I'll come back when you are.' To me it sounded disappointed and excited. It felt like it was silently telling me it meant that it was coming back when I was about to die. Scared the fucking shit out of me!"

Of course, in this book and concerning the alleged data regarding sleep paralysis, I am oversimplifying because I am here to discuss the spiritual aspect of what happens when we sleep and leave our bodies. Spiritually speaking, when we sleep, our souls leave our bodies, travel the astral plane and roam freely in and out of all different dimensions and realms. They would be extremely bored just sitting there idly all night long while the body gets the rest it needs. Spirit doesn't need to sleep, and neither does our soul, as it is, at its very core and essence, our spirit. Our souls travel to converse and commune with our higher selves, extra-dimensional beings, our angels and guides and even extraterrestrials. These otherworldly entities only understand the CONCEPT of emotion and are completely clueless, aside from on a very basic and scientific level, about the extremely wide range of emotions we humans feel all throughout the day. So while we sleep, we are oftentimes teaching these "others" why we made some of the choices we made throughout our day-to-day lives. They are fascinated by us and want to learn as much as they can.

As beautiful and enchanting as all of this sounds though, when we are sleeping is when we are at our most vulnerable. Not only are we not awake and therefore not aware, our soul is not in our bodies, and we are simply lying there for the most part unprotected. Entities like certain shadow people or the Djinn are oftentimes lurking and waiting for just these moments when we are helpless to stop it to make their move and try to jump into our bodies and take them over. Unless we are dealing with an actual demon whose mission it is to destroy the human, most of the other entities simply use us for food and want to feast on not only our fear but the pain and suffering we have the capacity to cause for others as well. They jump into our bodies, and they cause us nightmares and horrifying dreams where, even as we lie there asleep, our hearts pound and we are terrified. Have you ever started to doze off and all of a sudden you jolt awake with a start? This is your soul quickly jumping back into your body because it either knows you are going to wake up and wasn't prepared for you to do so, or it was jumping back in quickly to stop one of these entities from temporarily possessing you and causing you whatever low-level emotions it undoubtedly had in store for you should it have succeeded in its mission.

What about that paralytic state in between being asleep and awake where we are mostly aware of what's going on around us but unable to move? Sometimes we can move our eyes, but that's about it, and there's no way to scream or call out. There are so many different things people report seeing during these episodes, most of which we are in the midst of exploring right now.

There is a big difference between sleep paralysis and night terrors, with a night terror being when a person wakes up, usually with a start, in a state of complete panic and fear. It is also not the same thing as nocturnal fear either, as this is when a person wakes in absolute fear and downright terror and, despite knowing a nightmare or bad dream caused it, has no memory of it at all and is left to grapple with these horrific feelings, usually in the darkness of their bedroom, which makes it all the more terrifying. However, as scary and common as all of these things are, there is something that sets sleep paralysis apart from all of it. These are the entities that are said to be involved every single time.

I've come across such vast differences between what people are claiming to be experiencing during these paralysis episodes. The variation from encounter to encounter is almost overwhelming. Every once in a while though I come across two encounters that are so similar, I can't help but feel it lends even more credence to the idea or theory that something very strange and far out of the reach of the scientific realm and community is happening.

Here is another example of a shadow being or some type of supernatural force that seemingly likes to cuddle up and whisper sweet nothings into the terrified victim's ear. This happened to a man who says he woke in the middle of the night in a state of fear, panic and paralysis, only able to move his eyeballs. This is very common when dealing with this particular subject. However, he claimed that as he looked towards the bottom of his bed, he saw a creature hunched over that could only be described as looking like a female "Gollum" from the *Lord of the Rings* trilogy. This entity put one gnarled, long and gangly finger to its lips to shush him—as though it had no clue he was paralyzed and couldn't yell out—as badly as he wanted to. The entity then proceeded to climb over the bottom of his bed and into a spooning position behind him. As he lay there unable to move or call out, smelling a putrid scent he described as feces, death and sulfur, "she" laid one arm around him, snuggled her forehead into the back of his neck and then leaned up and whispered in his ear, "Go back to sleep." The voice was raspy and mocking, and suddenly he jolted out of bed and saw there was nobody and nothing there with him. He raced to turn on the lights, and once he did, he also saw the room itself was empty of any and all entities. However, he could still smell the rotting stench and could almost feel the thing's arm around his waist. He slept with the lights on for the rest of that night and invested in a night-light for the nights to come.

The plain fact of the matter is you only have to be human to be able to know when something is "off" and when something is in a room with you—regardless of the darkness or anything else that may be going on. This is why it's so easy for skeptics to dismiss claims of shadow entities and really any other supernatural and otherworldly events. They provide the absence of proof as the proof of absence. They have a much harder time disproving encounters where people are obviously hurt and even killed by such entities.

Chapter 5
Christopher Case

Christopher Case was an elevator music executive in the 1990s. In 1999 he lived in Seattle, Washington, in the 1300 block of North 152nd Avenue in North King County. He was described as a fitness buff, happy-go-lucky and easygoing, with tons of friends. Chris was extremely physically fit and took great care of his appearance. Despite his personality, good looks and great career, he was single at the time and preferred staying home by himself and just listening to ancient Egyptian music, which was somewhat of an obsession for him. He really wasn't looking for love or even to date anyone at that point in his life. Chris traveled a lot for work, and while on a business trip to California on April 11, 1999, he decided to go out to San Francisco with his friends, who were there with him because they were also his coworkers.

One of the coworkers decided to bring along a lady friend of his who was local to the area. This woman by all accounts was extremely attractive and described as "intense looking." She was about twenty years older than Chris, who was at that time thirty-five years old. The four of them talked all night, and by all accounts they had a nice evening. This unnamed woman and Chris found they had a lot of similar interests, including, of all things, ancient Egyptian music.

Chris was only looking at this woman platonically; however, at the end of the night, she asked if he wanted to go back to her place. Chris realized the woman was interested in him romantically, and he declined her offer, as not only was he not interested, but he didn't want to lead her on because he really did enjoy her company. She asked him again, somewhat pleading, promising that they could just sit and talk some more and listen to music. According to Chris (when he later recounted the story to his friends), after his second decline of her offer, she started getting super "pushy" and "aggressive." She kept insisting he come back to her place and spend the night, which made him very uncomfortable. He was trying to be polite to her, decline her offer in a nice way and not come off as rude, but the woman just kept pushing and insisting and wouldn't stop. She wouldn't take his no for an answer. Finally, Chris decided he needed to just make his exit. He told her and everyone else that he was just going to go back to his hotel and cheerfully said goodnight to everyone.

As he stood up to leave, this beautiful, charming

and friendly woman suddenly became visibly angry. She pulled Chris in close as he went to shake her hand and whispered in his ear, "I'm a witch, and I'm gonna put a curse on you, and you will die by the end of this week!" Although taken aback, Chris turned and left without another word. The next day, April 12,1999, he and his coworkers flew back home to Seattle.

Once Chris was home, he called a good friend of his named Sammy. Sammy was an old friend who was not only a teacher but also a psychic. Understand that Chris was, by all accounts, not superstitious or religious by any means. He called Sammy and recounted this bizarre encounter with this "crazy lady" that he had had the night before. Although he didn't even remotely believe in such things as curses, witches and spells, he did think it was extremely weird and wanted to talk about it with a friend. Neither Chris nor Sammy took any of this very seriously and chalked it up to a random encounter where maybe the woman just had too much to drink and was sensitive to being rejected.

About forty-eight hours after the encounter, on April 13, 1999, Chris later told friends he heard whispering coming from outside his bedroom, near the front door. Keep in mind he lived alone and didn't have any pets. Also, from the time he got home until now, everything had been perfectly normal and routine for him. He explained that he heard this whispering that was starting and stopping, but not being superstitious at all, he just chalked it up to him being tired and hearing things.

Once all the lights in his apartment were turned off and Chris had lain down in his bed to try to get some sleep, he heard the whispering again, but this time he heard it coming from all the way across the apartment. No longer from near the front door, but on the other side of the place altogether. He then started thinking that maybe someone had broken into his house and what he was hearing was a burglar. With this thought, Chris got up out of bed and followed the sound of the whispering into his laundry room, but once he reached the laundry room and flipped the light on, it stopped completely. Suddenly all was back to being silent again in the house. He didn't see or hear anything further at this point, so, laughing at himself for getting all worked up over what now seemed to be nothing, he turned to go back to his bedroom to go to sleep. This is when, out of the corner of his eye and in his peripheral vision, he saw a dark shadow run across the room, by his front door/kitchen area. This was where he had first heard the whispering coming from.

At this point Chris was really thinking that he was in fact being burgled and started turning on all of the lights in the house. This is also when he started hearing the whispering yet again, only this time it was coming from literally all over the whole apartment. He walked through all the rooms and turned on all of the lights because now he was looking for a person, an actual human intruder. A burglar. The whispering at this point was a bit secondary because he thought that the shadow figure he had just seen running past his kitchen out of the corner of his eye was a person, a human being who had broken into his home to rob him while he slept.

Standing in one place with all of the lights on, Chris could see the entire layout of the place and realized there was nobody there; the entire apartment was empty except for himself. This was when it occurred to him that he could still hear the whispering. It sounded now as though it was coming from his bedroom, but once he got there, he couldn't pin down where exactly it was coming from. And so it would go that if he thought he heard it coming from the bedroom, once he got in there to check, it would seemingly move and start sounding like it was coming from somewhere else in the apartment or stop altogether. Needless to say, Chris didn't get any sleep that night because the whispers never stopped all night, and he spent the entirety of it chasing them down only for them to either stop or disappear the minute he reached the spot or room where he thought it was coming from. Also, as he was chasing phantom whispers throughout his place, he was still seeing the shadowy figures in his peripheral vision. However, anytime he would try to look at them dead on or turn towards where he had just seen them out of the corner of his eye, there would be nothing and no one there again.

The next morning, on April 14, Chris decided to call Sammy. All of this information came from Sammy recounting to the police later on all the conversations she had had with Chris throughout this week. When he called Sammy, he was completely panicked like she had never heard him before as he recounted to her what had happened the night before. She later said that she was worried right from the beginning, from the first phone call, because it was just so incredibly unlike Chris to be freaking out about things like whispers and shadow people. It was extremely worrying for him to even be considering anything supernatural or paranormal because he did not believe in any of it. She described him as "terrified." He was a real stand-up guy and always so levelheaded, so he felt like he couldn't call the police because what would he tell them? "I'm hearing random phantom whispers and seeing shadow people in my peripheral vision"? He knew how insane that sounded.

Sammy tried to reassure him and just hoped that whatever happened didn't happen again. She was very concerned at this point, but eventually they got off the phone. Remember, this is the late '90s so there were only landline telephones when all of this was happening. That night—the night of the fourteenth, the same thing happened again in Chris's apartment. As soon as he turned off all the lights and tried to go to sleep, the whispering and noises would start up, and he had to get up and turn on all the lights and start hunting down where the sounds were coming from, but it seemed as though every time he got close to it, it disappeared or moved to somewhere across the house. Now keep in mind he was sleep deprived because he hadn't slept the entire night before, having been up doing the same exact thing, dealing with these whispers and shadow people running through his apartment. The difference this night, though, was that Christopher was able to see these shadows running around and saw that they were actually in the silhouette of a person.

Now, because everything was becoming more and more vivid as the night progressed, Christopher wasn't sure if that was actually a case of reality, that shadow people were really running all around his apartment, whispering to him all night long, OR if it was the lack of sleep from the previous night, which was making him have even more realistic delusions and hallucinations. He spent his second night chasing these things throughout his apartment and once again didn't get a wink of sleep.

The next day on April 15, Christopher decided to call a few of his other friends, who choose to this day to remain anonymous. According to what they reported later on, all of them had gotten the same exact account from Chris as Sammy had gotten the first night it had happened. They all said that basically no matter what was actually happening and no matter if they or anyone else believed it was happening, that Chris definitely believed it was happening and started spiraling very quickly after it all started. They concluded that whatever it was he either thought or was actually experiencing, it was terrifying him.

On the night of the fifteenth, Chris decided and was determined to finally get some sleep. He tried his best to convince himself that the events of the previous two nights were a result of stress and lack of sleep. He was basically trying to convince himself that it was safe for him to go to sleep, as he had been awake for more than forty-eight hours at this point and was admittedly on the verge of delirium anyway. Unfortunately, things were about to get much worse for poor Christopher Case. Eventually he was able to fall asleep, but he woke up in the middle of the night hearing whispering again. This time, though, he was completely and totally paralyzed. He couldn't move at all and knew right away that this wasn't sleep paralysis because, although he was totally immobile, he was also wide awake. Now remember, it was pitch black at this moment because Chris slept without a single light on in his whole apartment. The whispering started to move from outside his bedroom door to his closet and then to directly under his bed. He started praying that this was just a nightmare and that nothing bad was going to happen because now he was thinking of and worrying about these shadow beings that had been in his house the past couple of nights.

Suddenly, out of the corner of his eye, he saw something coming up from under the bed next to him. At this point he could only move his eyes. So he did. He moved his eyes only, and when he looked over, he saw one of the shadow figures appear right next to his bed. He couldn't see any features or anything, but he, from what he could glimpse at least, could see that it was one of the shadow/human-shaped things he'd been seeing, and it was right there next to his bed. This shadow entity was just hovering over Chris's paralyzed body. All of a sudden, while he sat there helpless and unable to move a muscle, the shadow thing reached down, grabbed a hold of Chris's neck and began to choke him. He was completely immobilized and therefore couldn't fight back or even struggle against the attack. The entity then started lifting him by his neck and off his bed. He had no concept of time and therefore never really knew how long it held him there for, but eventually, after a few minutes or possibly even just a few seconds, it threw him back down and then vanished into thin air. By this point not only was Chris gasping for air and struggling to breathe but he also still couldn't move. He just lay there, totally convinced that this thing was going to come back and kill him. He wholeheartedly believed that he was going to die that night, and he was absolutely terrified.

Eventually Chris somehow managed to fall asleep while still unable to move and terrified the thing was going to come back and kill him in his bed that night. When he woke up, he could move again, but when he did, he saw some kind of incisions on his fingers. Ten in total, one for each finger. The tip of each finger had been cut off. His hands and bed were full of blood, which we can safely assume was Chris's own from these horrible cuts he had apparently sustained while asleep that night. He immediately got up to look in the mirror because his neck was hurting. Sure enough, there were marks and bruises going around his entire neck, and it also looked as though someone had strangled him, just as the shadow person had done the night before while he was incapacitated.

This brings us to April 16, and Chris just woke up to these incisions and these marks on his neck. So the night before suddenly hit him all at once. He realized that everything that happened had ACTUALLY happened. It wasn't sleep paralysis; it wasn't a nightmare; it was now his reality! He was terrified and feared for his life.

He decided to call Sammy, and he told her what had happened. She said she was speechless. She later said he was so terrified and panicked that he could barely articulate what had happened and that if she didn't know Chris and his character, she wouldn't have believed any of it. (And that's really saying something because, remember, Sammy is a psychic.) She tried to calm him down and get him to call the police, but Chris knew that he would sound like an absolute crazy person, wondering what he would even tell the police if he did call them. "A shadow person who definitely wasn't human appeared out of nowhere in my room last night, tried to strangle me to death and cut up my fingers? Oh, and by the way, I've also been hearing random phantom whispering throughout the last couple of nights that I can't place where it's coming from." Chris decided that wasn't going to get him very far with the police even if he did call them, which he decided he wasn't going to do.

So finally it dawned on him: maybe that woman in San Francisco DID put a curse on him, and he decided that he wasn't going to take it lying down. He started to do some research. Chris was known as being a very reasonable and rational man, so in doing all his own research by himself, he thought he could avoid too many people knowing what was going on with him. He was very high up in his company and feared gaining some kind of troublesome or even crazy reputation for himself. He went to a local bookstore and obtained some books about demonic possessions, the occult, witchcraft, etc. He not only purchased a bunch of books, but he bought anywhere from ten to fifteen crucifixes.

After doing some research in his apartment, he ended up putting these crucifixes all over and in every room. He also poured salt along the baseboard in each room. He made one long line that wasn't broken but that just went in, around and against every wall. Chris then took the salt and poured a little pile of it into every corner of the apartment. In his utter desperation, he was doing everything he had read and heard that he should do in the case of demonic possession, entities attacking, witchcraft and spells. He just wanted to protect himself, at least until he could figure out not only what was going on but how to get rid of and/or stop whatever it was.

The very next night, April 16, Chris had just got done putting all of these protective measures into place, and honestly, nobody knows what actually happened to him that night. What we do know is that in the middle of the night, he went running out of his apartment in nothing but his boxers and checked into a hotel. The next morning, April 17, Sammy called Chris to check on him, and in 1999 remember, the only option was a landline call, and he didn't answer because he was at the hotel. However, neither Sammy nor anyone else knew that because he left in the middle of the night and didn't think or have time to tell anyone. Now keep in mind, Sammy had been speaking to Chris these past few days, and he'd been telling her and describing to her everything that had been going on, so when he didn't answer, she completely panicked and called the police and asked them to do a welfare check on Chris's apartment. His other (anonymous) friends were also concerned and agreed a welfare check would be the best thing.

The police went to his apartment, but all was quiet, and the place was locked up, so they told Sammy that nothing really seemed out of the ordinary and that the place was locked up tight. They also explained that they couldn't break down the door or otherwise gain entry just for a welfare check. Sammy lived all the way across the country and was completely panicked, but helpless to do anything.

Sammy went to work that day, and when she got home, she had a voicemail from Chris from earlier in the day when she was at work. Chris told her, in what she later described as a kind of defeated voice (which the past few days he'd sounded nothing but terrified), that he was under attack and felt he was going to die that night. He also told Sammy in this voicemail that neither he nor anyone else could do anything about it. He sounded like he was just accepting it, as though he recognized it as absolute. To him, or so it seemed, it was simply fate or fact. Sammy tried to call Chris back, but again, he was at the hotel, and though she was extremely concerned for and worried about her friend, she knew if she called the police back, they were most likely not going to go back to his apartment at all or at least not until the next day. Sammy then decided she would just let it go until the morning.

This brings us to the morning of April 18, seven days after he met the woman who claimed she was a witch and put a curse on him. Word got back to Sammy that morning that Chris had not shown up for work, and no one could get in touch with him or had heard from him all day. She decided to call the police back and explain the situation, this time including the facts that he had uncharacteristically missed work that day and that no one had seen or heard from him, aside from the voicemail she'd received the day before, in days.

The police went back to Chris's apartment and saw

that his front door was wide open. They walked inside to check everything out and make sure Chris was ok. The police later stated they weren't sure what to think when they walked into Chris's apartment and saw all of the piles and lines of salt, as well as the many crucifixes that were recently hung all over the walls. Chris had not gotten rid of any of those things because he was using them to try to protect himself from whatever was attacking him the past week. Police also found dozens of candles completely burned out and all these little messages scattered all over his house, which were later determined to be written in Chris's handwriting. They were allegedly notes that supposedly were to ward off demons, witches and curses, etc. After seeing all of these seemingly random and bizarre things in his apartment, they decided to just finish searching.

The last room they checked was the bathroom, and that was where they found Christopher Case's dead body. When they found him, Chris was fully clothed in a waterless bathtub surrounded by dozens of burnt-out candles and some more crucifixes. Also odd was Chris's position, as he was found on his knees with his hands in prayer position and pushed up against his chest. There were no obvious external injuries, and the coroner ended up concluding that Chris had died of "natural causes," mainly a heart attack.

Needless to say, his friends and family were not buying into this, and they tried desperately to explain to the police and coroner what Chris had been going through in the past week and everything that he was telling them had been happening to him beginning seven days earlier when he'd met the woman who claimed to have been a witch and allegedly cursed him. No information ever came to light about the woman who had seemingly put this hex on Chris, and no new information has ever been learned about this case. It is still considered a death by natural causes.

I included this case in this book specifically because it's the only case I have come across so far where I fully believe, as do many other people, that Chris was in fact killed by shadow people. Whether through the means of a curse or not and regardless of what the entity actually was. It could have been literally anything at all, but it chose to present itself to him in shadow during all of the harassment and each individual attack. This case has many facts and records that are available to the public. There's no denying what happened here, and it's one of the most terrifying cases I have ever come across because it took a young man's life.

Chapter 6
The Hat Man

The "hat man" is definitely something most of us have at least heard of, right? It's actually fast becoming the most commonly reported type of shadow entity sighted in the last twenty years or so. Reports of the hat man are indiscriminate in where they come from. If you've never experienced this entity, then let me describe it for you. Imagine, if you will, a humanoid, bipedal silhouette of a man that looks almost comically as though it has walked right out of an earlier decade and forgot to change its clothes. The era of the '40s and '50s seems to be its heyday, so keep that in mind as well as we move forward. That's the general gist of the hat man. The comic relief doesn't last long though as the terror and fear strike you to your very bones almost instantly upon laying eyes on the infernal being. The fact that the entity is all black yet dense, a complete and total "shadow," lends to not only its mystery but to the terror and dread it strikes into the hearts of those who witness it.

A highly esteemed expert on the shadow entity phenomenon, whom I mentioned earlier and who I believe is just absolutely brilliant, is Heidi Hollis. She wrote a book in 2014 based almost solely on this particular form of shadow entity, and it's titled *The Hat Man: The True Story of Evil Encounters*. She's collected more witness statements and encounters with this creature than I have, and that's really saying something.

Let's talk very briefly about one of the encounters in her book. It's enough to give you a general idea of what we are dealing with here. "Dear Heidi, I was maybe 5 years old when The Hat Man started to visit me. Every night I would lay in the top bed of my bunk bed and watch as my door would crack open for him to creep inside. As high up as I was, I would still have to look up to see him and I would freeze in horror at the sight of him." That pretty much sums it up, as anyone who has ever had the extreme displeasure of having an encounter with this entity will tell you. It's quite horrific and frightening to say the least.

While the hat man may seem to most people like just another shadow entity, there are some things that stand out about him/it that make me think he may be a separate entity all his own or possibly a leader of some sort with some form of dominion over the other—lesser—shadow beings. Most other shadow entities, even when focused on, are quite vague. This is why I am going through the different types with you here in this book. What sets them apart is how they behave. Even when you are able to focus on them really well, they have the same basic features. Not Mr. Hat Man though. He is not only consistently described as wearing some sort of hat, with cowboy hat, fedora or even a top hat being the main three, but of wearing distinguishable clothing as well. Many times he will be described as wearing a three-piece suit or a trench coat. I have even come across encounters where the witness swore they saw a pocket watch included in the ensemble, which he will glance at or even pull out of his pocket from time to time. The imagery itself evokes a deeply ingrained sense of terror inside me that chills me to my core.

We have already discussed the benign shadow people, and later we will even explore the rare occurrence of the shadow entities who are flat-out helpful. Again, it's hard to know what you're dealing with until they make their move. The hat man always brings with him a sense of fear, terror and/or doom. There has never been a case where a hat man has come and brought feelings of calm and serenity, wanting to make friends or being helpful. He is definitely evil all the time.

The opinion is almost split down the middle as to whether or not there is only a single hat man who terrorizes the entire world with his presence or if there are many entities who fall under this category and who simply all look exactly the same. I am of the opinion that there are many of them. If they weren't, for whatever reason, always only seen by our human eyes in shadow, I wonder if they would all look completely different. After all, if you found another long-haired woman who stood at five feet seven inches tall and had a total mom-bod, put her next to me and then turned off the lights—if you didn't know either one of us, would you really be able to tell the difference? Add to that the sense of fear and confusion that overtakes the witnesses simply by laying their eyes on it and then tell me if you would be able to tell the difference. The answer, most likely, would be a resounding no.

There are many people who believe as well that the hat man will almost exclusively visit people who are experiencing some type of lower vibrational or negative emotion to the extreme. For example, not only anger or sadness but downright rage or grief. While this is definitely a common thread in the hat man victims—whether they're aware of it or not—I do not think they are exclusively visiting people who are experiencing such major and acute emotions. I believe they are indiscriminate and that all shadow entities are here to feed off of all emotions, positive and negative. It stands to reason that the more extreme the emotion, the better the energy "tastes" or is absorbed by it. While this is certainly a common thread, it's common to all shadow entity encounters. Most people aren't that aware of their deep, inner emotions or feelings before the fear and dread these encounters and attacks bring about to be able to get any sort of conclusive data on this.

Earlier I touched on the possibility of telepathic communication between shadow entities and their victims, and here is another way in which this entity specifically stands out. The hat man is known to be quite vocal in his threats of harm and words of terror. He has no qualms about screaming in a witness's face or whispering in their ears. On the rare occasion someone does report a different type of shadow entity verbally speaking to them, it's always in some language that to our human ears sounds like absolute gibberish. Again though, the hat man is unique, and he very clearly and plainly says what he intends to say without hesitation. I've noticed as well that whatever language the witness speaks, that's the language the hat man speaks to them.

The hat man also has a different way of moving than his seemingly lower counterparts. While the other shadow entities are always reported as gliding or otherwise floating through the air, and even while seeming to be standing still are just hovering, the hat man walks like a human being and actually stands on the floor. This sounds reasonable, as he is sometimes not only seen with the aforementioned pocket watch but also tipping his hat to the victim as well.

Here is an example of an encounter with the hat man, which has all of the standard identifiable characteristics and more. It starts with a woman we will call "Meghan," who says she started being visited by the entity in 1978 when she was only six years old. Meghan grew up in Alabama and spent a significant amount of time that year and 1979 at her grandparents' house who lived in the same state. She, her mother and her sister lived with her grandparents on and off due to her grandfather being in and out of the hospital so much and the family not wanting the elderly woman to be left alone in the home while he was gone.

Meghan and her sister shared the only spare bedroom in the house, and when other relatives would come to visit, which happened often, the two would have to give up that room and stay in their grandmother's room with her. It didn't take too many nights of this for both of the young girls to understand they weren't alone and that something evil was lurking around. Meghan would sleep between her grandmother and little sister with her head at the foot of the bed. She recalls having a very vivid, recurring nightmare where, as she lay in the exact same spot she was sleeping in, she would awaken to the dresser drawers in the room flying open by themselves, with clothing and ghosts flying out of each one. This struck me immediately as uncommon because normally we dream of being anywhere other than exactly where we are lying while having the dream. Meghan's dream self tried to gently kick around in order to rouse either her sister or her grandmother, but neither would wake up. She states that in her dream she debated whether or not to walk into the other room and wake up her mother but decided against it for being fearful of having to walk past the dresser, which was directly next to the only door leading out of the room.

Dream Meghan looked away from the dresser and over to the window, and that's when she saw the hat man for the first time. Of course, she wasn't aware, at the time, of what she was seeing. The window was directly behind the headboard of the bed, and all she knew at that moment was that a very tall man wearing a hat was lurking there. At first, she thought the strange man was standing on top of the headboard, but as she got older and thought about it more, she realized that most likely "he" was just extremely tall, seemingly even more so considering she was only a six-year-old little girl.

This man was wearing a top hat, a long, flowing coat and was carrying a cane. She also explained that he had no real features and that, even though he seemed to be made of shadow, he still somehow managed to block out all of the light that was coming in from the window from the moon and other lights outside. Not only was she terrified because there was someone else in the room with her who definitely shouldn't have been there but also because she at once recognized him as nonhuman. The two locked eyes (or so it seemed with her only knowing where eyes should have been but seeing none) for what seemed like forever but was most likely just a few seconds, and then the figure lifted his arm and pointed right at her. It said, "This is your last chance." Meghan describes this interaction very well, and it's something that I have come across many times but with people being unable to fully get across what she is about to say despite their best efforts. She would say later that the voice didn't fill the room at all but rather was inside her head. "The voice was flat with no residual sound, as if everything surrounding the words had been removed." That was it, just five little words, and then the entity put its arm down and vanished back into the darkness.

The next day when Meghan told her family about the strange "dream," they chalked it up to a terrible nightmare and didn't give it any more thought. Meghan said that she kind of remembers being a little bit nervous when she had to sleep in her grandmother's room after that but only for a short time, and then she somehow forgot about it. Meghan explained that her whole family believed in the paranormal and were often swapping stories trying to scare one another or just creep the other person out. She didn't give the hat man or that encounter another thought until she was a teenager.

One night she was sitting around with her family, and they were all excitedly sharing their own paranormal encounter stories. Her mother, sister and grandmother were all there with her, along with one of her aunts. Meghan said that all of her family were spooked and fascinated by her encounter of that "dream" so long ago. However, her aunt didn't have the same reaction as the others and seemed to be almost terrified, as she turned a ghostly shade of pale herself and told of an encounter she had had, in that same house, of the same "man." The family was shocked, and they were all reluctant to spend any time in Grandma's room after that.

It brought Meghan back to wondering, though, as now that she is an adult, she realizes she wasn't dreaming at all and had had a real paranormal encounter with the hat man entity, what did it mean by what it said? She says the only explanation she could think of is that her grandfather had been in the hospital at that time and that he had died shortly after her encounter without her having seen him again. She feels that maybe the entity was telling her it was her last chance to spend some time with Grandpa before he passed. I do not believe this at all, but I will let you make your own decisions on it. Could he have been a friendly hat man who couldn't help how he appeared to this little girl? Doubtful as if that were the case and he could clearly speak English, then why not just come right out and say that she should go and see her grandfather? We will never know the real answers to this or so many other questions regarding this entity in particular or shadow people in general, but we can make our own guesses.

Chapter 7
Sleep Paralysis

A psychology professor at Northwest Missouri State University named April Haberyan claims that most encounters with shadow entities are probably the product of dreams (or nightmares). She explains that when people are sleeping and entering the REM phase, "It's common for them to see things." Essentially, she believes that everything involved in sleep paralysis, at least regarding the feeling of dread and even being attacked by shadow people or other entities, is all completely normal. "There are hormones in REM sleep that paralyze the major muscle groups and it's called 'paradoxical sleep.' Although this happens during REM, these people don't stay asleep, and the hormones are still in their bodies. It can last up to eight minutes and they feel pressure on their chest and can see people." This is insinuating that the entity will be gone once the person wakes up.

Don't get me wrong, this does happen, the person waking and the entity being gone, in some cases, but there are more reports than I could name where the person was fully awake and not in either REM state or between sleeping and waking where the entity, whatever terrifying thing it was in that instance, is still there and still very much attacking or otherwise terrorizing them. What about the encounters that happen in broad daylight while the person isn't or wasn't even sleeping at all or trying to? It's these encounters that make me push aside all scientific explanations altogether.

It's been said that approximately seven percent of the world's population will experience what science calls a sleep paralysis episode at some point in their lives. The encounters that come to me personally and that are all over the internet definitely make up a lot more than that percentage—and by far! It's true that during the REM phase of sleep we can experience dreamlike images and perceptions and that while half asleep we can trick ourselves into believing that an inanimate object we see every day in our bedrooms, for example, a coat rack, is some sort of entity there that's causing the paralysis we feel. Sleep paralysis is a real thing, don't get me wrong, but I just can't justify it being responsible for every single encounter I've come across where someone was attacked or terrorized by something in their environment that wasn't human and that definitely didn't belong there.

Scientists and experts on the subject say that the entities that are either seen or perceived are a result of subconscious dream activity and the body's inability to properly cycle through all of the sleep stages and therefore perceives, with any combination of the five senses, some entity like a demon or shadow person who they believe is there to induce harm. Okay, but if it isn't real, then why is it that what we are allegedly only perceiving is always there, in our minds at least, to hurt us? What about the people who have physical injuries and symptoms of attacks? Our mind certainly can't manifest the bruises, burns, bite marks, scratches and so much more that a lot of people wake up with after one of these experiences. While it's true that women are more likely to have an encounter episode, it obviously happens to men too.

Here's one of the many accounts I have come across that science blames fully on sleep paralysis and tricks of the mind. A thirty-five-year-old man named Mike who was married had been struggling with alcohol addiction for most of his life. He had had some clean time under his belt but always fell off the wagon and started drinking again. His tolerance was extremely high, so when he decided to stop drinking cold turkey, the withdrawal effects were too much for him to handle. This is why he always gave in and ended up drinking again—at least according to him. Mike enlisted the help of his wife, and through a referral from his PCP, he was able to get himself into a rehab.

He also had a history of severe panic attacks, which, in recent years to when this was happening, were becoming more frequent and increasingly more overwhelming. Mike told the psychiatrist while in the rehab that the panic attacks mainly started while he was sleeping or trying to fall asleep. The doctor determined that he was having episodes of sleep paralysis. Mike explained there was one specific entity he encountered over and over again during these episodes of alleged sleep paralysis. The entity was a woman who would always appear standing alongside his bed and who he believed had murderous intent towards him. Mike fully believed that it was this mysterious woman who was somehow immobilizing him and rendering him unable to breathe and who was paralyzing his muscles. Just like most other episodes of sleep paralysis, Mike was fully cognizant of the woman and could see her very clearly but couldn't move anything but his eyeballs. The woman was also allegedly choking him. As he tried to fight back and get her hands off his throat or, as he believed, stop her from killing him, he realized he was "rendered" completely immobile and unable to do anything but lie there and take it and pray he didn't die. This obviously put Mike into a state of very real and very severe panic—hence where the panic attacks while sleeping had allegedly come from. According to his doctors at least.

Mike claimed the attacks from this woman would last anywhere from two to six minutes. I just want to insert here that the average duration of most sleep paralysis episodes, including the attacks, last no more than eight to ten minutes, tops. This is where I start having problems with the medical and scientific community and their diagnosis and explanations. Mike was having approximately two to three episodes per year and had been having them for about nine years by the time he was admitted to rehab. Once he started receiving psychiatric help, the number of events increased to about two per week! This made him somewhat paranoid that something bad was going to happen to him while in the care of these professionals, and he started having terrible anxiety, which was accompanied now by heart palpitations and severe insomnia. So, basically—at least from my point of view, the alleged professionals here were making things worse and totally dismissing Mike's concerns. Also, they were blaming his addiction. According to one report, Mike was eventually able to overcome his fears, anxieties and even his addictions, but it is unknown if he is still having these rendezvous with the mysterious, murderous stranger in the night.

So-called experts explain that sleep paralysis is characterized by either a sensed presence, perceived fear or both, which they refer to as "intruder hallucinations." The inability to breathe that inevitably accompanies these sensations or "hallucinations" is called "incubus hallucinations." There are auditory and visual presences, which include but definitely aren't limited to hearing footsteps, sensing an intruder and seeing shadows. So, this all sounds just like the encounters with the shadow entities, and it would all make sense, and the neat little package they're trying to present to us to make us believe it's all in our minds—quite literally—would also make sense except for a few things. First of all, as I mentioned earlier, WAY MORE than 7 percent of the world has had these experiences. Secondly, none of this accounts for the aforementioned injuries, which are very visible, in most cases cause physical pain and that there are no other explanations for how they got them. Lastly, there is no actual explanation as far as I can tell (at least not one that seems reasonable anyway) as to why almost every single person has the exact same types of entities that they "perceive." Is it even possible for this many people to be having the same exact hallucinations, all over the world and completely independent of one another? I'm not buying it.

There's a couple of encounters I've come across in my research that I would love for the scientific community to try to explain away for me. One is the case of a young man who was asleep in his bed, which was right next to the door that led downstairs to the basement. He had just lain down to go to bed and wasn't even asleep yet. He had just closed his eyes when he heard footsteps coming up the basement steps. He turned to look but didn't see anyone, and the basement door was closed as it always was. The noise went away, and the boy closed his eyes again. He must've dozed off because when he woke up just a few moments later (he knew because he had his phone in his hand when he fell asleep), he heard not only footsteps coming down the steps, but as he listened closer, he heard breathing in his left ear. He was completely paralyzed except for his eyeballs, which I'm sure at this point were wide and bulging out of his head due to the fear and panic he must have been feeling. He rolled his eyeballs to the side, and sure enough, the basement door was open. There he saw a tiny little white-haired troll with a ghoulish face. The creature was grinning an unnaturally wide grin and staring at him, unblinking, and breathing heavily into this young man's ear.

Suddenly all the phones in the house started ringing, and it seemed as though the ringing got louder and louder as time went on. He was under the impression he would have permanent tinnitus and started panicking even more. You might be thinking this was a strange thing for him to be worried about at this moment, and we will get to that in just a minute. After several minutes of looking at this thing looking and grinning at him and listening to the symphony of cellphones and landlines build, he was finally able to wiggle his fingers. As he did this, the ringing stopped, but the troll was still there. He managed to lift his arm and blink, and when he reopened his eyes, the basement door was closed, and everything was back to normal. This encounter stuck out to me because the entity was more than a mere shadow and very visible, but that's not why I included it here. I brought this specific case to your attention because of the thought process that this man was having during this entire thing. I believe these entities—whether shadow, demon, troll, etc.—are there to feed off of us and purposely put these fears in our heads. Since this troll creature realized possibly that it wasn't provoking enough fear in and of itself, it amped it up a bit and made the guy panic that he would have permanent damage to his body once he was able to move again. I just don't see the scientists convincingly explaining away all of this.

I'm not saying I don't believe sleep paralysis exists or even that it's never responsible for hallucinations, but to me it's just not reasonable that it is the explanation for every single encounter ever had throughout time and the world over. There's just no way. In some countries they refer to a sleep paralysis episode by saying, "the dead man got on me." This explains it all in a nutshell, really. This is exactly how most people claim to feel when they are in the middle of an episode/attack.

The first known scientific description of what we have come to call sleep paralysis dates back to the year 1674 and to a Dutch doctor named Ijsbrand van Diemerbroek. The phenomenon at this time had taken on the name "incubus," and that word was gathered from the mythology popular in Europe in that day and age and since the beginning of the Middle Ages, which meant a demon who perches atop a woman while she sleeps in order to have sex with her. Now we know that, while incubus and succubus entities do visit us in the dead of night and often while we are sleeping, these can be a part of, be separate from or have absolutely nothing to do with a sleep paralysis encounter. Just like we here in the paranormal community feel as though we have come a long way from using "incubus" as a scientific theory or reasoning on what sleep paralysis actually is, so does science. They now say that it is neurological misfiring while we sleep, and the main causes of it are, in order, not getting enough sleep, sleeping on your back, being extremely stressed out mentally, not being on a regular sleep schedule, and/or having a sleep cycle that is for whatever reason constantly disrupted. Examples are someone who works an overnight shift or new parents.

While we may not ever know what sleep paralysis actually is and whether it's paranormal or supernatural in some way, I am fine here on the fence of whether or not I believe all experiences with it are one thing or another. I believe it is a mix of science and Spirit, of energy and misfires and of light and darkness. Speaking of complete and total darkness and adding in a bit of chaos brings me to thoughts of the Djinn. Let's get back to the supernatural now, shall we?

Chapter 8
The Djinn

The Djinn are the shadow entities who are the most feared and who have the most somewhat definitive information circulating about them. They have a backstory and a whole history that goes back to the beginning of time. The Djinn are ancient and extremely powerful and should definitely be avoided at all costs and whenever possible. There are a small group of Djinn that are said to be sometimes friendly and helpful, but much more often than not, they are dangerous and manipulative and not something you would want to take a chance with in order to determine which type you are dealing with. I fully and wholeheartedly believe they are parasitic in nature and feed off of our fear and any negative energy we may experience or any lower vibrational feelings we may have such as sadness, depression, hatred and fear. Another word we use for this in this community is vampiric. They are definitely, among other things, energy vampires.

One of the most respected and learned researchers into energy-based spiritual entities is a woman who unfortunately passed away named Rosemary Ellen Guiley. She knew her stuff and wrote the books *The Vengeful Djinn* and *The Djinn Connection*, among many others. She was absolutely brilliant, and I will miss hanging on to her every word while reading her books. She said many times about how the Djinn feed on things like, "They can eat human food when they take human form, but our food does not sustain them. It gives them pleasure. They can absorb the essence of food, and things like the molecules from tobacco smoke, which provide enjoyment. Their main source of nourishment is the absorption of energy from life forms. The best is the draining of a soul, but is difficult to do and is considered unlawful. It is, however, practiced by certain powerful, renegade Djinn. The vampiric absorption of the life force can be quite detrimental to people, and cause health problems." Before I try as best I can to unpack that statement, I would like to first discuss the history of the ancient Middle Eastern Djinn.

We have always had a particularly disturbing history with these entities, and according to ancient legends, they were here long before us. At the very least they were tens of thousands of years ahead of us. The sacred book of Islam and its teachings is called the Quran, and in its pages you will find a very detailed history of this supernatural energy-based entity. Those of the Muslim faith believe this holy book is the word of God, like the Christians believe in the Bible. Of course, He is called Allah to them.

As someone who spent a lot of time studying all different kinds of religions while trying to find where I fit in the grand scheme of things and what I truly believe, I can tell you, and if you too have studied the Quran and the Bible, you will already know, that despite there being many major differences in these two holy books, there are also so many deep similarities as well. In the Bible it teaches that God created the human race in the form of Adam and Eve. Eve was crafted from one of Adam's ribs. In the Islamic teachings of the Quran, Allah not only brought Adam into creation as well, but here there is so much more to the story. He brought humans and the angels to life and created them and us, but he also created something else. These are supernatural entities that had the same status as the angels. The Djinn were made of smokeless fire, but despite their being so powerful and mighty, things took a bad turn for them fairly quickly after the creation of humanity.

In the Quran it says that the angels and the Djinn were ordered by Allah to not only respect but to show a deep reverence for Adam. The angels obeyed; the Djinn... not so much. They made the catastrophic decision to go against Allah's mighty word. They were immediately cast aside and unceremoniously flung out of the realm of heaven with their only shot of maybe redeeming themselves not coming until Judgment Day. This is when they will be given the chance at regaining their higher-up status (while still having to respect and somewhat bow to us humans). On Judgment Day, a day that no one knows when it's coming, the Djinn, or so it's said, will be lined up before the Creator and have the chance to make amends and apologize for going against His mighty word and disobeying His orders. They were, or so it seems from all of this, the original rebels without a cause—but with a (very sinister and evil) cause. Until that day comes, though, for some reason that I still cannot come to terms with or make any sense of at all, these entities are allowed to not only freely roam the earth and the spirit realm as well, completely doing as they please when, where and how they want, but we are somehow and for whatever reason—most of us anyway—helpless to do anything about it for the most part.

Their activities include feeding on us, making our lives miserable, physically harming us and possibly— and this has happened; it's documented throughout history so many times—killing us. They are able to do great physical harm, and as a matter of fact, this is the entity I wholeheartedly believe stalked, haunted and then killed Christopher Case—at the behest, of course, of some evil witch he refused to bed. Here's the thing though, when it comes to physical violence, as I stated—they are extremely capable and more than willing to hurt and even obliterate us, and I doubt they even give it a second thought after feasting on our fear and death and doing only God knows what with our immortal souls afterwards. They are even able to influence us to commit terrible acts, but only to a certain degree. They can influence but never compel. We have the final say, of course, mainly because of the free will we were given, but I mean, who stands a chance when you have a Djinn influencing you to not only make poor decisions but also to commit acts like taking your own life or the life of someone else and committing violence against others as well?

According to the legend, the most powerful of all the Djinn is Iblis, and he is their overlord. The name Iblis literally translates to "despair" in English, so that right there should speak volumes. Iblis' objective is comparable to Satan's, and in fact, they could kind of be considered one and the same in that it's his job to lure the human race into sin and essentially over to "the dark side." Iblis is also called by the name Shaitan, and it's said that he is "the ultimate Djinn" whereby any other Djinn are like Satan's demons and therefore his minions to do his bidding. Obviously if you know anything about the Christian Bible, you will see the similarities here. Iblis is the one who ordered all of his fellow Djinn to disobey and revolt when they were ordered to bow down to Adam by the Creator. Iblis saw himself, the other Djinn and even the angels as far above humanity and scoffed at the idea of ever bowing to us and, in fact, thought it should be the other way around.

In stature the Djinn are also much bigger and larger than us. Iblis' reasoning for his beliefs was simple in that it went back to what each of us was created from—meaning the Djinn and human beings. Man was made from simple dirt, and the Djinn from smokeless fire. The Djinn are more powerful than us, and their lifespans are considerably longer. From a simple human's perspective, the Djinn are basically immortal. Iblis and all other Djinn too are shapeshifters, and some of the forms they're able to take on are extraterrestrial, a large black dog, elementals and snakes, to name a few. They're also able to come and go interdimensionally as easily and as quickly as we are able to snap our fingers. So it's true that in some ways the Djinn are technically superior to us, and when in their presence, it's just as easy for them to manipulate us as it is for them to switch the aforementioned dimensions.

I really hate the fact that, in today's society and especially in this community, the nature of the Djinn has been not only watered but dumbed down and simplified. Calling a Djinn a genie or relating them to one is not only false but extremely dangerous as well. The Djinn are not some mythical, happy-go-lucky, wish-granting cartoon character but are instead some of, if not the most fearsome and terrifying, evil and cruel, supernatural and often demonic entities out there with very few exceptions. They can and do, very easily, intrude upon our world and instigate hatred, havoc, murder and mayhem when, where and how they choose.

So, what about their "lives" and domains? It's been

universally accepted, at least by those who follow and believe in the Quran, that the Djinn were made from smokeless fire. If that's the case, then you may be wondering how they are so easily able to feed off of human energy the way that they do. How can they have a physical form, an intelligent consciousness and perform what I'll put in extremely simple terms and call feats of "magick"? Most likely, the references to the Djinn being born of any kind of smoke or fire has been accidentally misinterpreted over time.

Rosemary Ellen Guiley believed she had the answer to these seemingly unanswerable and nonsensical questions. I believe the conclusions she drew were correct as well. It has to do with what we call plasma. She suspected that the Djinn are actually plasma-based entities and that this is what caused the misinterpretation of the "smokeless fire" creation story. She also posited that both the realms of heaven and hell mentioned and agreed upon in both the Quran and the Bible are dimensions of existence most of us have no access to and that are extremely different from our own three-dimensional world. That's an understatement to say the least. She stated, "These different aspects are what govern the universe, the fundamental forces of nature, and all the elementary particles contained within." As most of us probably know by now, heaven and hell are just two out of an innumerable and possibly infinite number of realms beyond our own. The Djinn most likely inhabit many of these realms only they are not of flesh, blood and bone like us, despite seeming to be so when we come into contact with them, but of plasma.

Despite the insurmountable number of seeming differences between humans and the Djinn, there are some things about us that are similar too. They marry and have offspring, and they have male and female entities. Remember, too, the Djinn only seem immortal when compared to our human life spans, but they do in fact eventually die. While they inhabit a completely different plane of existence than our own, they technically also inhabit the same one. For example, if you think you are alone in your bedroom and you're just hanging out, watching Netflix or talking on your phone, there's always the chance some sort of entity from somewhere else is sharing that space with you. However, just like the Djinn, they are able to eye your every move and listen to your every sound while also remaining hidden from you because they don't fully cross into your space. This is why so many people who experience supernatural activity or what we call hauntings always describe an odd sense of not being alone or even of being watched. The laws just work differently for other dimensions, and from what I surmise, we have the most restrictive dimension and also the most restrictions too, meaning in our physical bodies and what we can not only do but perceive with them.

The Djinn are known to have a love for music and oftentimes will whistle a tune to keep themselves entertained. Our early morning hours are the hours in which they're the most active in our realm. If you are ever startled awake by random whistling or the humming of some hypnotic and seemingly foreign tune —you most likely, unfortunately for you, are dealing with a Djinn. In many cases they only just seem to be passing through. When they leave their own dimension or plane of existence, the Djinn are said to dwell in deep underground tunnels, caves and in the remains of abandoned and/or broken-down old human structures. Nowhere is this more apparent than in the Middle East. It is true for the whole world though, too. They prefer ancient Indian and Middle Eastern music, but again, that's based on the specific tastes of the individual entity. All are said to absolutely love the sound of the sitar though.

They have a love of dogs, and our canine friends can easily spot a Djinn and, as we know, other entities as well, when we can't. Dogs and donkeys are said to be the ones who will spot this particular entity the fastest, though, as they see them even without them having to fully cross into our dimension.

When going back to how they have been called genies in our western culture, I think this stems from the fact that the Djinn are well known for offering the people they're torturing some sort of gift or trinket. It's also true you can make deals or barter with them, but as we all should know by now—when you deal with a devil, it seldom turns out in your favor or good for you at all. So, along those lines, imagine trying to cut a deal with THE devil and see how that works out for you. I won't hold my breath waiting for you to get back to me on that one after you've tried it. The deals and offerings of gifts and trinkets is most likely where the genie and the three wishes scenario came from though.

The Djinn are, more and more as time goes on, able to enter into the minds of those they are targeting. Being a Christian, I immediately thought of demonic possession, and I wasn't too far off when I started researching further. The overtaken or "possessed" person can then be made to do all sorts of things that, unfortunately, our closed-minded society will blame on mental illness or the afflicted person just being evil and psychopathic to name just a few modern labels. I am not saying these things or this type of person doesn't naturally exist. I am just saying that it isn't ALWAYS the case.

Most of the time the Djinn torture, manipulate and haunt us for the simple fact that they can and that they like to. It really is that straightforward. A lot of the time though they simply play tricks on us and love to manipulate electricity. They may move things around or hide things in your home and make you drive yourself half-crazy searching for the hidden or moved item and wondering how in the world it ended up where it did. They can blow up your lights and make your appliances fail to work with no explanation over and over again. The only motivation the Djinn have for interacting with us is the absolute delight and pleasure they get from manipulating and tormenting us. There really is no other motive. Other than, of course, to feed off of our lower vibrational feelings such as fear and anger to simply name a few.

They cause not only mental but physical illness as well, and I'm pretty sure this is where the feeding comes in. Rosemary Ellen Guiley warns us, "Their main source of nourishment is the absorption of energy from life forms." Rosemary tells of many encounters, but one that stands out to me, and also that deals with what's thought to be a "simple shadow person" is that of Emily. In 1999 she lived in Texas and had an encounter with a "shadow entity" in her apartment. Many people who know better, though, believe she was encountering not only one Djinn but several of them. She had recently, as in just a couple of weeks before the encounter, become interested in and started researching the Djinn phenomenon. This in and of itself should be a warning to us to be careful what we start looking into lest it start looking into us. Just thinking about them too often could open a doorway that allows them in and causes them to focus on you. This is not the case with all supernatural entities but definitely the Djinn, the MIB and the BEK, just to name a few. These are the ones we should try not to even give a second thought to once we come across them— as hard as that may be for some of us.

Emily lived in an apartment in Texas back in 1999. She claims that after starting on her second book about the Djinn, she started to see, out of the corner of her eye, small shadow-like figures lurking all over the place. She would peripherally see them behind couches, standing in corners, and peering around doorways. She also felt they were pulling at her duvet at night while she lay in bed, trying to sleep. Innumerable electricity outages like her alarm clock and microwave not working all of a sudden and out of nowhere. Aside from all of these things, she was having nightmares of the Djinn, in which it sucked her energy out of her directly mouth to mouth in some sort of backwards resuscitation exercise. I couldn't find out how things ended for Emily, and it really could have gone either way. I am assuming it couldn't have gone that bad, as she was around to tell her story.

Something to always keep in mind is that the Djinn, and really any supernatural or otherworldly entity, are nothing to play with or joke around about. This is especially true if you don't know what you're doing. Leave it to the experts and try not to even research too much into certain things on your own. If you're unsure, ask an expert and take it from there. While not every single entity that appears to us in the dead of night out for fear and terror who wears a dark, hooded cloak is a Djinn or even a shadow person at all, I feel like enough of the time they do fall under this category, and that's why cloaked, hooded figures do not have their own chapter here. They could be demons or even the Grim Reaper as we have come to know him, but the important thing to remember is this very big difference—shadow entities ARE the shadows, whereas other entities simply try to hide themselves within them.

Chapter 9
Pets/Ferals/Cats

There are a couple of kinds of "animal" shadow entities I have come across. The ones that seem to be an entity all their own (mainly cats, for example) and then there are the ones that are the reason I use the word "pets" to describe them, as they are always accompanied by a human-shaped entity. I have even come across encounters where this seemingly lesser entity looked as though it were on some sort of leash being held and controlled by the humanoid or shadow "person." These types also seem to possess even less of a human personality than their larger counterparts although most of the time I have seen them behaving in exactly the same way as a normal pet would while on a leash. Overly excited and seeming to jump around and pace back and forth. It is almost as though they are actual animals who got very excited once their leash went on because that means it is time for some fun.

It's been said that only after attaching to people

do shadow entities start to be able to exhibit complex behaviors and take on more "humanness," if you will —that being more of a human personality. I don't even know what to think about this alleged observation, as I have trouble with understanding how someone could analyze such a thing, especially to the point where they feel confident enough to allege they have data regarding the specifics.

The lone standing, catlike entities seem to be a form all their own. Most of the time they haunt specific places and seem to go out of their way to suddenly appear beneath your feet, perhaps trying to make you lose your balance and fall over, possibly hurting yourself or worse in the process. These entities will show up even in a fully lit room and appear as a shadow on the wall. I have noticed that aside from the aforementioned tripping attempts, these cats are normally there to torment your pets.

We all know by now that animals, specifically domestic cats and dogs, are almost always much more sensitive to the paranormal happenings of a home than the humans who live there. I have a friend who had a cat named Lily for years. Lily was a nasty, ornery black cat that one couldn't even walk past without getting hissed or swatted at. Lily's claws would always be out, and even my friend couldn't pet her. I questioned why she would keep such a nasty little beast around and care for it so well when the thing would just as well see her dead than allow her the smallest bit of affection. This question didn't go over well, but I still wonder what the appeal of Lily was. Lily eventually had to be put down though, for one reason or another I can't remember.

After this, my friend got herself a little kitten, black as midnight just as Lily was, and this one was exactly the opposite in not only its behavior but mannerisms as well. Whereas Lily would growl and hiss at everything that moved in her orbit, this little kitty is skittish and seems to fear everything. She spends most of her time hiding in the other room under a bed when I visit my friend, and after my experience in that house with Lily, it's all the same to me.

The last time I was over there, my friend asked me if I could put out my "feelers" and see if there was something going on in her house because while her new kitten is a scaredy-cat during the day and during waking hours, it seems as though the second all of the lights are off in the house and my friend lies down to sleep or even just turns down the lights to watch some TV, this cat acts like a crazed lunatic. She bounces off walls—literally. She meows loudly, hisses and scratches up the furniture. She jumps all over the tables and chairs, knocking things down as she goes, and sometimes she even jumps into bed and cuddles up with her human, shaking and seemingly scared out of her wits. Perhaps from interaction with some unknown and unseen entity or force. My friend isn't sensitive at all and didn't notice anything strange going on but was concerned enough she started wondering if maybe she was missing something or if, perhaps, something was there that she couldn't see, simply to torment her cat.

My first thought was that Lily's spirit was back and being spiteful towards the new, shyer and much sweeter kitten that took her place. I never expected what I found. I stayed the night and saw that there was another animal there, torturing this sweet little thing, but it wasn't Lily—it was a shadow-cat. This thing, which I had never personally encountered before in all of my years of doing this, showed itself to the both of us as we sat and watched television that night. We saw the shadow of a small cat on the wall in front of us, behind the TV. We both assumed it was the kitty and thought nothing of it. Suddenly though we heard kitty start hissing, and when we turned to look, she was arching her back and staring directly behind the television where there was the shadow of a cat. It wasn't hers though. It was extremely clear it was a whole separate entity too because as I said, the "real" cat was now hunched over and growling, and the shadow cat was simply sitting there.

The next thing we knew, kitty struck and jumped at the wall, almost knocking herself out in the process, and the shadow cat took off at a much higher rate of speed and disappeared somewhere into the darkness of the next room over. While all of this seems very comedic, I assure you when it is happening right in front of your face, it's not only fascinating but terrifying.

Some people who have episodes where they are being attacked by shadow entities and can't move have even reported seeing what looked like a cat sitting on their chest. They were being held down by its massive weight. This doesn't make sense, at least not according to our laws of physics, because no cat would weigh enough to be able to sit on a human's chest and make them literally not be able to breathe or move—but it's happening in so many cases. This is another way I'd like to point out that we can prove all of these entities have density and aren't simply weightless shadows and that's that, for example, when dealing with one of these cat shadows, as I mentioned earlier, we can trip over them. I've heard people tell me they were tripped down or up the stairs by a randomly appearing cat in the middle of broad daylight, and also I've been told on more than one occasion how a cat shadow was walking along on someone's mantel, and as they sat there thinking they were going crazy and should possibly have their eyes checked, items from the mantel started falling over one by one as the shadow cat seemed to bump or touch them.

There have been hundreds if not thousands of encounters now where people claim to have been held down by a shadow being or an old hag creature during an alleged sleep paralysis episode, so why are the shadow cats only there sometimes? Are they used to instill even more fear? I'm not sure and am still searching for more on this particular entity. They're faster than anything we humans are accustomed to seeing move, and they are like their humanoid counterparts in that, sometimes at least, you may only see them as darting past your peripheral vision—only much closer to the floor. I suggest being extremely careful where you step should you even think you might have one of these entities in your home. They aren't exclusive to tormenting animals, but it is ALMOST always the case—provided they aren't sitting on your chest, that is. It seems pet owners and non-pet owners alike have been subject to this bizarre brand of torment over the years.

Let's move on to the ones I liken to "pets." I had my first encounter with one of these types very recently as well when, on my first night staying in my mother's new house back in June of 2021, she woke up screaming as she was being attacked by a shadow entity. She explained that before she noticed the entity that attacked her, she saw "some sort of animal with a fuzzy tail that was on a leash" running back and forth at the foot of her bed. This was creepy on so many different levels, especially considering I was lying in the same bed as her when this happened.

As I did more research, I came to learn that this is almost always the case, with the pet being spotted first before the actual entity itself. It's almost as though these things are some sort of distraction for when the being wants to get in real close to the human and doesn't want to be seen doing so. Yes, it's true we wake up to them on top of us, choking us and committing all sorts of other atrocious abuses, all the time. I'm not sure what the difference is here and/or why the "pet" is needed. I only know that they seem to be for something, in some cases.

I've also recently come across a bunch of encounters where little kids and adults alike were seeing these pets and somehow getting it into their head that this was a pet of theirs that had recently passed away. Therefore, they want to play with it, thinking that it is their beloved old pet that they are still mourning.

I should insert here that in the case of the seemingly leashed shadows, they're different from the cats in many ways but mainly in that they look like the shadows of dogs. Again, not always, but most of the time. It seems as though these "pet" creatures add a whole new layer and dimension to the fears already struck up by your average shadow entity. I don't have enough encounter stories or data to even begin to try to understand whether or not these shadow cats and dogs/pets are evil, benign, serving some purpose for their humanlike counterpart or something else altogether. I mention them though, as I am sure by the next time I get to discuss this subject with you all, I will have more answers because the experiences are becoming more and more common the more I research them, though still seemingly with no common thread.

As I'm sure you've noticed, I didn't only include cats and pets in the title of this chapter and for good reason. I have come across so many different shadow animal entities I would be able to put together one heck of a shadow zoo if I were to be able to get all of these animal entities into one place at one time. There's one encounter that really stood out to me as more bizarre than average that I would like to include here if you'll humor me for a few more paragraphs. Though there may be several encounters of this type, the one I bring to you now comes from my home state of New Jersey.

A forty-three-year-old woman and her new husband moved into their very first home and were looking forward to spending their life together in beautiful Cape May. Neither one of them had ever had any type of paranormal or supernatural encounter before, and things like this weren't even on their radar aside from in the scary movies they both enjoyed watching but put no real stock into. Oddly enough, the couple lived in their house for almost four years before anything strange started to happen. It started off in a very weird way as well, with strange yet delicious smells wafting through the house randomly, even when nobody was cooking or baking.

As they sat one night and watched one of their favorite horror movies, they both looked at each other, and the woman asked aloud if her husband was smelling the same thing she was. It was the smell of fresh-baked blueberry muffins, and it was so intense and strong a smell it even seemed to be overriding the smell of the bag of popcorn that sat between them in their laps. Though it smelled good, it was very much out of place, and because this wasn't the first time they had encountered something like this, they were a bit concerned. This wasn't a smell like something that could be wafting in from a neighbor's window or something either, as it was almost midnight and the summertime. The air conditioner was on, and all of the windows were closed. The husband admitted he was indeed smelling the exact same thing, and because this had already been happening for months, though the smells varied from fresh-baked cookies to apple pies and even breakfast foods such as pancakes and waffles, they were concerned and intrigued enough to get up and investigate. The couple wasn't sure exactly what they thought they would find or even what they were looking for, a phantom baker didn't seem very reasonable to their logical and rational minds, but it surely wasn't what they found, that's for sure.

The couple followed the smell to their basement door, and when they opened the door to further investigate, the smell disappeared just as quickly as it had come on. They were both a bit creeped out at this point, though neither could put their finger on exactly what it was that was causing this feeling, so they both went back to the movie they were previously watching and decided to forget about the whole thing.

A few days later they had guests over for a BBQ, and the woman's mother decided to stay the night and help clean up after all the other guests had gone home for the evening. Once she went into the guest room and the couple retired to their own room, it was only a matter of minutes before all three of them were in the hallway, trying to follow the random scent of cinnamon that seemed to have permeated both of the rooms being occupied. They all looked quizzically at each other, and the woman explained to her mother that this was what she had been trying to tell her earlier, as she had briefly mentioned the strange smells that sometimes wafted in, seemingly on a phantom breeze, only to disappear as quickly as they came on.

The woman's mother suddenly looked as though she were stricken with fear and muttered something about going back to bed and turned and did just that. The woman herself was freaked out enough by her mother's behavior that she turned and did the same, but the man simply couldn't ignore his curiosity this time and decided to investigate. Once again he ended up at the basement door and opened it. He went down the stairs, and the strange and delicious smell seemed once again to just evaporate into the thin air it seemingly originated from. This time, however, he continued on down the stairs.

He pulled the string for the very dim, hanging light that was just above the bottom of the stairs, and immediately he saw something out of the corner of his eye. When he turned to look, whatever it was seemed to stand perfectly still as though, like we discussed earlier, it thought that perhaps it wouldn't be seen if it didn't move. What he saw confused him at first, and it took a few seconds for him to understand what he was seeing. It was a shadow approximately two feet tall and standing on four legs. It had what looked to be a long, slim tail, which seemed to be swaying back and forth. It was an animal of some sort, but which kind he couldn't be sure, as it was only a shadow. He could make out no gender or facial features and couldn't even be sure if it had fur or not. It seemed as though he had been staring for quite a while, but as he remembers it now, it couldn't have been longer than a second when the thing took off to another, much darker and unlit corner of the basement and disappeared into the shadows there. The man didn't wait around to see if it reemerged and took off running back up the stairs.

The next day he told his wife and mother-in-law about what he had seen, and they both thought he was pulling their legs. It wasn't long though before his wife at least would change her mind. After about a month or so of having no more experiences with random smells or shadow animals, she went downstairs into the basement to get some clean clothes out of the dryer. As she did so, she pulled the light switch at the bottom of the stairs, and there stood, directly in front of her, the same shadow thing her husband had described to her the night of the BBQ. The thing took off the second she laid eyes on it, again into another corner where it wouldn't be seen, and she, as her husband had done before her, hightailed it back up the stairs without even grabbing her laundry.

As I sat and spoke with them about these bizarre encounters, I could see that the sense of fear this topic brings up in them is overwhelming, particularly for the husband. They never spoke of it again, and the woman waits until daylight to do laundry going forward. They still live in the same house (this all took place back in 2009), and though they've seen what seems to be a swaying tail out of the corner of their eyes from time to time, always accompanied by the smell of fresh-baked and delicious treats, they just do their best to ignore it. According to their logic, if they ignore it, it just might go away. I didn't bother to try to convince them otherwise, as I am always envious of people who are able to do things like completely ignore what's right in front of them. I see it as a sort of self-preservation I just wasn't born with.

At the end of the day I asked what in the world they thought they encountered, and they said they didn't know, but it really looked like the shadow of a monkey. Only, of course, there was no monkey anywhere near their home and especially not in it that would be casting a shadow on their walls. I was also curious about this alleged smell that came along with it. This is why this is all so incredibly interesting to me as well, despite how silly it may sound to some people. I mean, I have heard of all different kinds of horrible and rotten smells accompanying many things that go bump in the night, and the shadow people are no exception, except never such sweet, delicious and seemingly enticing smells as those reported here. I hope to have more information soon on these animal-like shadow beings. They absolutely fascinate me, and though they seem to invoke a fear in the person witnessing them, it seems as though they are almost always being used by a bigger entity for some nefarious purpose like distraction or to invoke more fear for feeding off of.

Chapter 10
The Lurkers and Observers

The lurking shadow entities or "the lurkers" will do just that. They are most often found in the bedrooms of homes and tend to remain in the shadows of the room, in the dark of night, just staring at their human victim. I have heard a lot of alleged experts explain that they don't believe these particular entities have any real intent and are just observing. However, because I separate this entity from the observer, I can tell you I beg to differ. Perhaps creepiest of all about this entity is that it doesn't exclusively lurk in corners of the room, it seems as though that's only what it does when you're awake, and there's the real possibility you will see it, head on and ever so quickly, before it slinks back into the shadows. You will be left with no doubt about what you saw and almost certainly filled with fear. This usually happens right before bedtime and leaves you with a sense of overwhelming fear, dread and confusion, which are all lower vibrational emotions and feelings. Why is this important? Because all three of those are what shadow beings and entities like them feed off of the most.

I believe these lurkers are the more dangerous of the two when compared to the observers because when they allow you that quick glimpse of them, it reminds me of when someone is marinating meat. Trying to let it sit and absorb whatever it is so that it is tastier when it's time to eat it. We are left after such encounters to lie there in the darkness of our bedrooms, turning over and over again what we just witnessed when we laid eyes on the lurker. It'll be near impossible to fall asleep, and once we are either almost sleeping or lying awake but with our eyes closed—that's when the entity strikes. It will then suddenly be standing and lurking right over your bed. Oh yes, this thing is doing way more than observing, it's preparing you and then sucking you dry as you open your eyes and see it there. You could possibly be in a state of total paralysis and unable to scream or move, or you could be so scared that when you open your mouth to scream, nothing comes out.

As with all other shadow entities I have come across and across multiple encounters, it is almost certain that if you are sharing a bed with someone, even the screaming won't wake them up. Mind you, this doesn't happen in every single case, but it's almost as if this entity just plays with you and makes sure to derive maximum terror from you as it stands there, possibly leaning a bit, right next to your bed. I must also point out here that this is much different from the observer, who is usually seen standing at the foot of the bed, and when you open your mouth to scream, you can, and the person next to you will certainly wake. Then the observer will disappear into thin air again, and you are left to deal with what you just saw.

Both of these entities have the basic humanoid shape commonly reported in shadow people encounters, and sometimes they even wear clothes. The hat man is never simply a lurker or an observer. I would like to further clarify my conclusions with an example of an encounter of each of these entities, and then you will see the differences I am speaking of without having to go down the extremely long list of what's the same and what isn't. I find encounters to be more entertaining than a bunch of listed statistics in most cases.

Some people will say the most benign cases are those of the lurker and observer because they both simply look, and though you may be in that state of paralysis or panic, they don't necessarily attack you. Isn't it true though that the psychic attacks, mainly in the form of sleep paralysis as we have come to know it, are in essence a physical attack as well? The body can't move, and the mouth can't make any noise. That sounds like an attack to me if I ever heard of one. Both the lurkers and observers can seem very benign, but again, because they feed off of us, they aren't even close.

Psychic attacks can cause all sorts of physical ailments and emotional disturbances, and I truly believe that every once in a while, a particular human becomes the focus of a particular shadow entity, and feeding on the human while they sleep isn't enough. This is when the entity will literally attach itself to the person and continue to feed, invisibly, throughout the day. This is very common for lurkers and one of many other reasons I chose to label it as such. It's not the entire, very tall and sometimes clothed being, mind you. It's mainly the essence of it, if that makes sense? You would certainly know if a shadow being were attached to you, or so you think, because you would see it; only that isn't the case either. They can very easily attach a part of themselves to multiple people and come back together when the time is right to feed the shadow body and then separate off again, onto the respective humans, and continue to feed until something stops them.

My theory on this was backed up after I read the book *Dark Intrusions: An Investigation Into the Paranormal Nature of Sleep Paralysis Experiences* by Louis Proud. He posits that sleep paralysis is perhaps a kind of cousin to spiritual mediumship in the way that possibly the experiencer is actually receiving a "visit" from an entity that is always amongst them. Where the person and the entity would almost always be locked in a state of mutual ignorance. Neither one sees the other. However, once they become aware of us, because they are of a lower vibration, they will latch onto us and feed off of our essence and life force energy. In my experience, to stop or detach them usually requires bringing in a healer of some kind or by doing the work yourself after you're sure you have one of these extremely overwhelming and oftentimes relentless entities attached to you. I'm getting ahead of myself, as I am going to discuss attachments in a later chapter.

For now, let's look at an encounter I came across where the victim at first had experiences with an observer but then after a while began to have them with what I believe was a lurker. This is not uncommon for shadow entity encounters to start off very benign, and then as time passes and they get more accustomed to your reactions and energy, you will then be visited by many other types of the same being and much more frequently. It always leads me to wonder if in fact it is different beings coming along as time goes on at all, or if it's the same exact being, but it was perhaps given a promotion or something. An even more terrifying thought is that maybe there actually are no individual types of entities and that all of them are all the others. What I mean by that is they can switch up which they would like to be as they please. I've come across a few bits of information contrary to this theory but not enough to make me throw it away completely.

Our witness, whom we will call "Janet" for the sake of anonymity, says she first started having experiences with shadow entities when she was only four years old. (Side note: I've noticed that age four is common across the board for people who have these experiences throughout their lifetimes as the age at which they claim to have seen their first entity. This is common in cases of all paranormal experiences with the age of four being given as the start of it all. I often wonder if it's really the beginning of it or if age four is just when most people begin being able to recall memories. My very first memory is my fourth birthday, and that's also my first memory of seeing a full-bodied apparition.) It started out harmlessly enough and also, quite randomly and with no warning, rhyme or reason as to why.

As she lay in her bed at night, once all the lights were turned off, she all of a sudden started to feel as though she were being watched. When she would open her eyes and scan the darkness of her room, at first, she wouldn't see anything amiss or out of the ordinary. It was only on the nights when she was alone in the room and never when she would have friends over or when her older sister was in the room with her. It seems her sister had her own experiences and was always afraid to be in her own room and at the age of ten started sneaking into Janet's bed at night because of it. It was an almost nightly occurrence. The girls weren't the only ones who noticed that Janet's bedroom was always several degrees cooler than the rest of the house, and her father even went so far as to call in a professional, on multiple occasions, to check that the thermostat or heater wasn't broken down in that one room. It was always perfectly fine, and Janet's parents kind of shrugged it off.

One night when her sister was away for the weekend at a slumber party and Janet was all alone in her room, all tucked in for bed and after her mom had just turned out her light, she started to feel a strange and now somewhat familiar feeling start to creep over her. She knew she was being watched, yet she tried to ignore it because every other time this had happened, when she had opened her eyes to examine her room, she seemed to be all alone in it. It seems either ignoring it simply wasn't going to work this time for some unknown reason or, and I am more of the latter opinion, the entity felt some type of way that she would dare try to ignore its presence, and things got really scary for the little girl and very quickly.

Suddenly the covers started being slowly pulled off her, and she felt her back start to get cold. She once again tried to ignore the feeling, possibly hoping with all her might she was simply imagining it, and she simply pulled the covers back onto her. The feeling of being stared at grew more and more intense, and Janet decided to try to hide under the blankets, again with the hopes that whatever was going on would simply stop. She said it was like she could almost FEEL someone or something standing over her and staring at her. It wasn't just the presence in the room that terrified her, it was the fact that she knew that it, whatever it was in this case, was focusing very intensely on her. Janet was now curled up into a fetal position with the blankets over her head and her eyes shut. However, the very second she opened her eyes, even though she was still completely underneath her covers, all at once they were ripped off her, sheet and all, and they landed silently on the floor at the bottom of the bed. Janet's eyes shot open, and there she saw a very tall, slightly muscular, humanoid, all shadow being standing at the foot of her bed and just staring at her.

She screamed, and her mother came rushing in, but by the time she got there, the thing was gone. Janet tried to explain what had just happened and why her blankets were on the floor, but her parents thought she was either just having a bad dream or possibly making up a story so she would be invited into their bed because she was lonely in her room without her sister. Her mother fixed her blankets, checked the closet and under the bed, and turned around and left the room. Within seconds of closing her eyes again, Janet knew the entity was back, and by now she says she was so upset from her parents not believing her and so scared of the blankets, which were now in her four-year-old mind a sort of barrier from the entity, being pulled off her again, she opened her eyes and faced the shadow person. As she lay there trembling and with tears falling down her face, it leaned in and put its face directly in front of hers to where if it had had a nose, it would have been touching hers. She squeezed her eyes closed again and started to pray, and after another few seconds, she knew she was alone in her room again.

This went on for the next thirteen years. Her sister eventually stopped sleeping in her room most of the time, and Janet never knew when the entity would come and pay her a frightening visit in the dead of night. When it did, it was always the same—Janet would immediately sense its presence and open her eyes, and it would lean in close for just a few seconds, seemingly enough to make her cry and tremble in fear, and then it would disappear back to wherever out-of-this-world and possibly demonic place it had come from.

As she got older, she felt as though it was the house that was causing the phenomenon, as she and her sister had finally talked about the nightly visitations. Her sister told her she had been tormented for years, and they both realized they were having the exact same experiences. They felt as though they were being examined. They also noticed that when the visits to her sister stopped completely, they began in Janet's room much more frequently.

When she was seventeen, Janet had the opportunity to move in with her boyfriend, and she took it. She said she was desperate to escape that bedroom and whatever was lurking there in it. Her words, not mine: "whatever was lurking." Within a month of living with her boyfriend, though, all hope of having rest-filled nights without this entity were dashed when, one night after her boyfriend was sound asleep next to her, Janet had just closed her eyes. She immediately felt the familiar feeling of being watched in the bed and tried to shake her boyfriend to wake him up. She was scanning the room as she did this and saw nothing, but she knew the feeling all too well to ever be fooled into thinking her old lurking friend wasn't there. Her boyfriend wouldn't wake up no matter what she did, and as she turned to lie on her left side, facing away from him and towards the bedroom window, she noticed what looked like dark feet beneath the curtains between the floor and where they ended. She screamed to it, asking what it wanted and yelling for it to go away but to no avail. She was crying and shaking but closed her eyes nonetheless; she said it was like being four years old again and hoping with all her might that the thing would simply get bored of her not paying any attention to it and therefore go away. Her boyfriend slept through the yelling and screaming and didn't wake up once that night.

This same experience would happen for the entire six years she and her boyfriend lived in this apartment. He didn't believe in such things as the paranormal or demonic and would make fun of her whenever she brought it up. Because of this, she eventually stopped telling him about it. She explained it was only once a month, and it would only be the entity behind the curtains. It never showed its full form to her, but she always absolutely knew it was watching her, especially when her eyes closed. She knew for sure it was there and not just a trick of the light or a paranoid mind, but because once she had gotten the courage to just squint her eyes open the slightest bit to see if it would come out from its hiding spot behind those long curtains. It did, and she saw it was standing next to them, perfectly still and seemingly facing her. It was simply observing, watching her as she slept.

What exactly was Janet dealing with here? We know for sure it was a shadow entity but what kind? Of the types I have come up with, it seems, as I previously stated, it was the lurker at first and then later on the observer. I thought this odd because I always thought these things got progressively worse, but it seems it went the other way in this case. It was pulling the blankets off her when she was a young girl, but as an adult it simply watched her. Was this the same entity? Was it two different ones? I have absolutely no clue and can only make an educated guess. I believe it was two separate entities that terrorized Janet, and I also believe that they were somehow in cahoots with each other. Each getting what it needed from her in its own way.

The lurker, by pulling off her blankets and confronting her face-to-face was eating up her fear and terror. I also believe it fed on her sadness at not being believed by her parents and her heartache from them leaving her alone in the room even after she insisted there was an entity in there and she felt unsafe.

The observer was simply making his observations. What observations and for what purpose? I'm sure I don't know, and the answer to the second part of that question will come in a later chapter when I talk about what I believe are the "time traveling" shadow beings.

While all shadow beings could very easily blend in with the shadows around them or the darkness of a room, it's important to note that they will always stand out if you know what to look for. As we discussed earlier, they all have density to them and, therefore, to the trained eye, can't hide so easily. Once you have had one experience with them, you will most likely be on the lookout from there on. Fearful to close your eyes at night and constantly scanning the darkest corners of your room. There are types of shadow entities that can and oftentimes do blend in very well with the darkness of their environment, and those are the ones that appear in the form of masses and mists. Dark as the inkiest black you can imagine. As dark as, some might say, the depths of a never-ending abyss.

Chapter 11
Black Masses, Mists and Blobs

When beginning my research into these particular types of sinister shadowy entities, I thought for sure the information would be scarce at best. I was wrong. These amorphous and oftentimes nebulous entities are a lot like their humanoid, bipedal counterparts in that they like to skirt the periphery of our vision. When seen clearly, however, they tend to leave us just as confused, terrified and with more questions than we already had from dealing with said counterparts. Something about the fact that these entities have no shape, at least one that isn't familiar like the human-looking shadow man/woman, makes them all the more sinister and terrifying. It's frightening trying to imagine a world in which these things, which give off a strong feeling of doom and oftentimes terror, roam freely. Are they somehow related to the humanoid shadow beings? To what extent and in which ways? I perceive them as a possible cousin entity. Maybe.

These blobs and masses seem to be after the

exact same thing—our fear and our essence, but they go about it in a much more terrifying and therefore much more efficient way. Most witnesses I've come across online or whom I've interviewed and otherwise spoken to in person have all described it as not quite knowing whether or not they were looking at something akin to a ghost or an actual shadow person. It's almost as though they're some sort of mixture of both all meshed up and blended together. This makes me very nervous because shadow people/entities in general are so incredibly unknown to us humans, so coming across something that we think might be one is enough to put anyone in a perpetual state of creeps. For whatever reason, these particular types of shadow beings make me think of the demonic.

One fascinating encounter comes from a woman who says she moved from her home in a small town into a large apartment in a nearby big city with some friends. This witness says that almost immediately she started to notice these strange and creepy entities. It started off with the entities darting around all over the floor. Back and forth as if bouncing off of the walls somehow, from the hours of just about dusk until ten p.m. However, as time went on, she started to see them more and more until it became a regular and somewhat ordinary occurrence. They initially began as pitch-black, amorphous blobs but over time shifted into all different types of other shapes and sizes. Also, as time went on, they seemed to have gotten bolder somehow, morphing from random blob to humanoid form and back again in the blink of an eye. Eventually her roommates saw them as well, and this was when things started to get really scary.

It was about six months into living in the new apartment when all of a sudden, the things got bolder and actually started approaching the humans. They never got close enough to be touched, nor did anyone try to reach out and touch them, but it seemed as though they were extremely curious about something or someone in the home. The more fear felt by the occupants of the apartment, the bolder these entities got, and the more terrifying they seemed to become. They all thought perhaps there was something in the water or the air that was making them have some sort of rare but serious group hallucination. Our witness explained that that's how quick the sightings would be. The entity or whatever you want to call it would be there just long enough for the human in the room to be aware of their presence and what they were seeing. Then suddenly they would either disappear altogether either into the ether or back to wherever they had come from, or they would morph into tiny little balls of dark mass and start bouncing all around the room again. It was enough to drive anyone crazy!

Once the pets in the house, mainly the cats and dogs, started reacting to them, the humans couldn't try to pin it on coincidence or the air anymore. They knew what they were seeing was real, and it was something they couldn't explain and were collectively petrified of. When it came to the cats, the blobs changed themselves into a shape almost identical to the animal and seemed to torment it as it chased it all around the house and across the rooms. The same thing went with the dogs in that the blobs would transform in the blink of an eye into a "dog" itself and dart about while the pet barked and growled incessantly.

One of the roommates who came forward had a slightly different experience in that she said she usually only perceived the entities in her peripheral vision and stated, "Sometimes I get to see them almost straight on yet I can't quite seem to focus somehow because they move just fast enough to stay out of the direct center of my vision." Right away this made me feel as though these things most likely are sentient beings of some kind. I mean, for them to know and understand that the peripheral vision was meant so humans can detect movement out of the corner of their eyes and out of their direct line of vision. However, it isn't meant for us to see any details, and therefore it is much easier for a victim to convince themselves they are just seeing things when whatever it is sticks solely to the peripheral vision.

The group tried to find out as much information as they could in the hopes of coming across something that would help them to get rid of the entities altogether but had no luck. The roommates, though admittedly very frightened, described the entities as giving off a neutral vibe and not seeming to be spiritually aggressive. They insisted the overall feeling when they saw these things was that they were merely curious. I would have to call that sentiment into question for the simple fact of how they seemed to interact with the animals in the home. They seemed to be aware of exactly what they were doing and how they were causing the animals to behave, yet they continued when it seemed they could very easily just disappear themselves back to wherever they came from.

While the entities seemed to be fairly benevolent—at least to the humans who were around—this is a very rare case. In fact, more often than not and nine times out of ten, these things strike fear and terror into the hearts of all who see them. People who are more sensitive than most to these sorts of things even claim to get an "evil vibe" that emanates from these beings, and that's said to sort of stick to the human who is witnessing it.

There is another man I recently spoke to while researching for this book who told me that he was having trouble with "a black dot" that would constantly appear, usually in the dead of night, on his walls. The dot would start off about the size of one of those laser beams used to drive cats crazy, and then as the witness would watch, and as his terror grew, so did the size of this perfectly round-shaped THING as it stuck to his walls. It would even show up in the bedroom while he was wide awake, and more often than not, it seemed to like to appear on the bathroom shower curtain while the man was behind it taking a shower. This was very interesting to me in that it stands to reason that the longer a witness is focused on this particular type of entity, the more their fear and terror would grow. Hence the reason, possibly, for the rapid growth of the entity. Instantaneous feeding! Where are we more vulnerable and caught off guard than in the privacy of our own bedrooms or in the shower—presumably naked—and washing ourselves?

After it would grow to about the size of a regulation basketball, it would shrink down little by little, just as it grew, and disappear into the wall or back into wherever it had come from in the first place. The man questioned how it was possible to see these things when it was pitch black in his room at night when he lay down for bed. While I don't yet have the answer to this particular query, what I do know is that this is exactly what most witnesses report; they say that even though it was a shadow and all black, it wasn't like a regular shadow, and it was somehow darker than the darkness of the room. I likened this to the color "off white." It's kind of white but not really. Basically, it's a bit "off." The same goes for the blackness of not only these shadow dots and blobs but all shadow beings collectively in that they are very dark black, but when it comes to actual darkness in a pitch-black room, they are a bit "off."

There is, of course, an alleged spiritual meaning to all of this as well, and I would be completely remiss in my objective of enlightening you, the reader, even as I learn as I go along myself, if I didn't at least mention it. Though this a gross oversimplification, it's said that these beings are the literal opposite of light, and it's thought that anything light is good, and anything lacking or being without light completely must be evil. It's wise to never think of things in terms of such extremes and absolutes, usually. I always try to see if there's some type of gray or in-between area, but in the cases of these black masses and blobs, I kind of have to agree that they're all malevolent in some way, shape or form. I am fully aware that black wisps of smoke that appear during certain spiritual rituals are simply the visual manifestations of the power of the moon and even the representation of the divine feminine, but this is not what I am talking about here. These entities are pure evil, and before they're even visually spotted, any person within their general vicinity will know that they're there and know that they don't have any good intentions whatsoever. That's pretty terrifying if you think about it, a being or entity that is so incredibly evil that you don't even have to lay eyes on it to know it means you nothing but harm and can possibly, very easily kill you.

The black-eyed kids are another great example of this. The sense of fear and almost primal dread that comes over a person due to what seems on the surface to be something as simple as a couple of innocent young kids knocking on your door. It's said that the minute you hear the knock, your heart starts to pound, and you simply cannot ignore the fear and

Gemma Jade

terror that is immediately struck into your heart and very soul. Right into your bones. I have been fortunate to never have had an experience with the BEK, but I have heard the stories, and I have seen the eyes of the people who have encountered them, even briefly, and it's something I will never in my life forget. The same goes for almost every single type of shadow entity I have ever come across, and these mists, masses and blobs are no different.

Many people have drawn the conclusion that shadow people in general are demonic. I am not so sure. It's said by so many that the Djinn are a kind of demon, but I believe they are something far worse. I never associated shadows or shadow people with demons or demonic activity before coming across this one encounter. It made me question everything I thought I already knew about each phenomenon individually. I always thought, "Why take the form of smoke or mist when your actual form is a demon?" It just didn't make sense to me or seem very practical when considering what all of these entities are out for in the end—maximum fear. However, this encounter really made me think about that sentiment long and hard because when I read it, I was struck with a deep sense of dread and unease simply from imagining what this witness went through. Picturing it in my head brought on the same panic and fear that is always present when encountering any sort of shadow entity. By whatever name we call it, that's whatever it is at the moment. Our witness tends to think his shadow encounter was with a demon, and I'm really not sure what to think. The encounter was sent to me by a man whom we will call "Ted" and who, in the early '90s, was living with his elderly mother in a house they shared somewhere on the east coast of the United States.

Ted seemingly all at once discovered a deep interest in demonology and all things occult. He saw a television show where alleged exorcisms were being performed, and before he knew it, Ted couldn't get enough research done on the subject. He would feverishly read about encounters and theories and everything else he could get his hands on almost from the time he woke up until the time he went to bed at night. Eventually he was blowing off work and his friends and even showering and eating less. He was raised in a very religious home, and his mother was growing more and more concerned by her son's strange interests as the months went on. While Ted never went so far as to disrespect his mother when she voiced her concerns, he did ignore her altogether and continued to hardly ever leave his room except to go to the local library to get more research. He even lost his job but was so enmeshed in the occult and demonology research he hardly noticed. He didn't realize it at the time but now understands this had become an obsession for him and that he couldn't have stopped if he wanted to.

One day as he sat there writing and researching all things occult, he noticed a subtle shift in the atmosphere of his room. He said it became unnaturally cold and dark and that the energy just somehow felt heavier. It was even harder for him to breathe. He figured maybe it was just that he hadn't opened the windows in a while and decided to finally take a break and shower. The room's atmosphere stayed the same though and actually seemed to deteriorate even more over time. It was all things he could live with and really didn't think much of. However, after about a year of almost every single day researching and investigating these evil and satanic topics, Ted said things got very scary. It happened so slowly and over such a long period of time it seemed almost like some sort of grooming being done by this entity and possibly even some other unseen forces as well, and until one night, it didn't occur to Ted that anything was different let alone wrong. It was as though, perhaps, the entity was taking the space over little by little and over time so as for it to be much less noticeable a shift when Ted finally did start to understand what was happening.

On the night when everything changed, he said he lay down for bed and noticed the room was even colder than usual. It was also much darker. There was light coming in from the outside, but it somehow didn't seem to be penetrating his room the way it normally did. After all, having lived in this same house and this same room his entire life, he was used to what was normal and what wasn't by now. He says as he closed his eyes to go to sleep, the feeling he had been feeling of being watched grew with such intensity he jumped up, expecting to see some intruder standing at the foot of his bed. There was no one there, or so it seemed at first. He did see a strange, circular-shaped shadow in the corner ceiling of his room that seemed to grow larger with each passing night. He explained it was unusually dark and inky black and that by a week since it had first appeared, it was now much larger and scrawled halfway across the ceiling of his room. It was no longer just a small dot in the corner anymore. He experimented with moving the furniture all over the place all of the time because his logical mind was thinking there had to have been something in his room that was casting this bizarre and somewhat creepy shadow. He kept rationalizing day by day as the anomaly kept growing larger night by night.

Ted stated, "It seemed to get a bit bigger. Confused, I moved some things around in my room, figuring again something in there was casting a shadow, to no avail. The shadow stayed the same, and although I was a bit disturbed by it, I figured there was a scientific reason for it—something outside was casting the shadow—and I would go to sleep like normal. Then, one night as I turned out the light and went to bed as usual, I noticed the shadow seemed bigger than normal. I repeat, this was a very strange shadow. It seemed to be 'thicker' than a normal shadow, almost like a puddle of black coffee. As I lay there, trying to fall asleep, but feeling very uncomfortable for some reason, I began to notice that with each opening and closing of my eyes, the shadow would loom larger and appear to be seeping toward me. I was frightened, of course, yet intrigued. It seemed the longer I kept my eyes closed, the quicker it would move toward me, but it would always stop right where it was whenever I opened my eyes. At one point, the thing was at the foot of my bed. I opened my eyes to look at it, expecting it to pause there. At this point, I was becoming increasingly frightened. Instead of pausing, it began to 'pour' toward me, and I felt the most unnatural empty, cold, hungry evil I've ever felt in my life come from it. It was then and there I knew for sure in my heart it was a demon, and I knew that it had relation to the junk I was studying. I pulled the blanket over my head, switched on the Christian music station, and prayed like crazy."

According to Ted, these measures worked, and the shadow-demon thing was gone for good. He also gave up his research into the occult and rejoined society again. He gained employment, made peace with his friends and moved on to have a productive and average life. I don't think Ted really understands, still to this day, that he was on the verge of either being overtaken, for whatever reason, by an evil and determined shadow being or full-blown demonic possession. We must always remember to be careful when dealing with anything involving demonic entities and the occult in general and to protect ourselves. This doesn't mean that reading a few books or watching a couple of videos on the subject is going to bring you to the brink of possession, but when it becomes an obsession as it had for Ted, that's where the danger lies. Also, some people are more susceptible to things like demonic possession because of certain attachments they may have or things happening in their personal lives at the time when they may be doing some research or whatever it is. Be careful.

Though I am still up in the air with my opinions as to the connection of shadow entities and demons in general, I do know that the research into them can cause very strange things to happen if it isn't done in moderation and with good intentions. I'd rather be safe than sorry, and because of Ted's and other encounters I've come across in my research, I just take extra measures of protection—in case what I'm dealing with, though maybe not a demon, has some sort of evil or demonic nature. We must never try to guess the intentions of entities that are around us, regardless of how good or bad they make us feel.

Chapter 12
The Astral and Time Travelers

Admittedly these are two very different types of shadow entities, but I combined them here because I do not have enough information on either one to give it its own chapter. First, let's discuss the possibility of these entities being some sort of astral traveler. I briefly mentioned earlier that there are extremely malevolent types who lurk in the shadows between realms and dimensions, just waiting for an unsuspecting person to either purposely or accidentally move into a state of altered consciousness. Here though, I am going to bring your attention to something a little different. The idea is that perhaps the spirit, while it is in this state and is traveling this way, for whatever reason, appears to those of us just going about our everyday lives as the humanoid-type shadow entities. Maybe this is the only way the conscious mind can perceive the spirit while in an unconscious state. I will continue to stand by my opinion that each entity is something different entirely. Though I firmly believe every form of shadow entity out there has some form of evil intentions, here is where the exception to that rule comes in for me. We can use the process of elimination to consider which entities would fit this particular heading and which ones would not.

The Djinn are entities, though shadow figures/shadow people, that we know a good deal about mainly due to their religious connections. Because the humanoid shadow figures who fall under the astral traveler heading almost never give off any sort of malevolent vibes, we can also eliminate the hat man. It would be unwise to base figuring out which type of shadow figure you're dealing with by intuition or gut feeling alone, even if you are sensitive, and that's because so much is unknown about them, and we are unsure whether or not one can convincingly appear as another altogether, but it's as good a place to start as any. Obviously too we can eliminate pets and amorphous entities. This leaves, almost exclusively, the typical and quite run-of-the-mill at this point shadow people.

While the humanoids are known far and wide to cause the same terror and foreboding feelings of evil and doom as their many counterparts, there are a few encounters, like the one we discussed in the beginning of the last chapter, where a person has said that they did not feel as though they were in any danger and that they felt that the entity was merely curious. Again, I will be oversimplifying here, but take for instance a man named Walter Rawls and what happened when he started experimenting with a certain area of the brain and recording the effects.

Walter placed a mask with monopolar magnets over the area of the brain known as the pineal gland, or third eye, in order to try to stimulate it and see what would happen should he be able to get it to be more opened up. Not very long into starting this experiment, Walter, who was placing this mask on himself and recording the data of what he personally experienced, started to notice something that at first scared him out of his wits. He started to see what he was perceiving as a shadow person, which would appear suddenly and seemingly out of nowhere somewhere in his room and then, after walking across the room completely, would disappear again right into another wall of the room. The entity would come in and randomly vanish into thin air, and the whole time, every single time, as it happened more than once, Walter said the entity never seemed to be aware that he was even there in the room with it. As the experiment progressed and over the course of a few weeks, Walter said that the entity became more defined and also would show up more and more often. Eventually it even seemed to be aware of him, as it would turn its head and glance towards him from time to time.

A man named Jerry Decker wrote about Walter Rawls's experiment in his book called *Interdimensional Shifts*, and in it he explained, "The third week, while busy working on documents, Walter noticed a change in the room. When he looked up, the wall had dissolved away, and he was looking at a small hill where a man and woman sat beneath a tree. It was the same ghostly male figure who he had seen on the other occasions. He sat quite still, watching this pastoral scene for several minutes. He somehow understood it very clearly and without a doubt that this man was most definitely the shadow entity that had been appearing in his room, mainly during his experiments, for the past few weeks. The man looked over toward Walter and appeared startled. It was as if he clearly SAW Walter this time and possibly recognized Walter as the ghost that he had seen the previous week! The image faded away and the wall immediately restored to its normal condition. From that moment on, Walter never used the pineal stimulator again."

I believe Walter was on the cusp of figuring out what some of these encounters with these specific types of entities really are. This seemed to have scared him, though, and surely I don't know why. I find it so incredibly fascinating, and I'm not sure I would have been able to stop if I had tried. This, of course, does not give us all the answers, but I do believe it takes us at least one step closer to understanding at least something about one particular type of these entities. However, I will be the first to admit how dangerous this is because, again, imagine if we thought that every single shadow person we encountered was simply a human being we were only able to perceive in shadow for whatever reason but from some alternate dimension or reality just like our own. Then again, the glimpse he got before he swore off this type of work for good was so incredibly small that how could we make any assumptions at all about what it was he witnessed on that last day? As far as I can tell, nobody picked up this work where Walter left off, and we are no closer to understanding anything more about these or any of the other types. Still, though, I thought it worth mentioning here.

Could it be as simple as just that? These shadow people appear to us in shadow as some sort of ghost or specter but who also perceive us, at the exact same time as we are seeing them, as the exact same thing? In other words, are WE the shadow people to someone else in some other realm or dimension somewhere? Do our paths cross simply because of some sort of "glitch in the matrix"? I'm sure I don't know, and while I know there is so much we can learn from this particular experiment from Walter Rawls, I regret to admit that, as someone who is more familiar with the paranormal rather than the scientific end of things, I can't even begin to imagine what any of that is or could be.

It's almost the exact same theory for those who believe that shadow people are some sort of time travelers as well. It's said that this theory mainly belongs to those who tend to take a more scientific approach to these types of things, but I emphatically disagree, as I believe this is a very likely explanation for at least the humanoid "people" types. Not the explanation for all of them, mind you, but at the very least some of them.

It's important for me when dealing with these specific types to really pay close attention to my own energy. Sure, I feel a great amount of fear when I see any sort of shadow being, but that's a knee-jerk reaction because of what I've been through with them throughout my life. I must look deep within myself and try to understand why I am so scared. Is it a deeply ingrained and somewhat primal fear, or is it simply that it's a shadow entity in general that's making me feel this way? It's not often I come across the latter, but it has happened once or twice, and I thoroughly believe that that is because these entities mean us no harm and are simply there to observe or collect data on something or other.

However, it's said that perhaps they either purposely present themselves as shadow like this for unknown reasons or possibly so that we don't recognize them. Perhaps it's actually the human eye that is to blame, and this is the only way in which we are able to perceive them. This will come up again when we get to the extraterrestrials, so bear with me here. Could it be simply the nature in which they are traveling here that makes it so that they cannot fully materialize in their natural form, whether that be human beings or otherwise? Some speculate that it isn't the vehicle future time travelers are using to bring them back in time that's making it so they can't fully materialize properly but whatever mission they are on instead. Maybe they are visiting certain places and times for very specific reasons and collecting data. Another theory that's just as plausible is that whatever benign-seeming shadow person you come across is the future you or someone you know, and that recognizing this would cause some sort of damage in the allegedly already fragile space-time continuum. Could it actually tear the very fabric of our universe for our future selves to have contact, even if it's just visual, with our "other" selves?

There is a major distinction between the "time traveler" shadow entities and the ones I simply call "travelers" in that the travelers seem to just be where you are but with seemingly no knowledge of or interest in anything around them—including humans. They travel in your peripheral vision but most times seem to be pacing back and forth before disappearing into a random wall or piece of furniture. Could any of the above-mentioned entities be interdimensional travelers and visitors? There are many string theorists and mathematicians out there who believe that there are at the very least ten other dimensions out there besides the one we all reside in right now. At most, at least as far as they can all tell right now, there are twenty-six! These "travelers" are constantly on the go and move with a sense of urgency. Oftentimes they seem to walk right past you without so much as a glance. These types have been known far and wide to walk through people as well. These entities are indiscriminate regarding day and night and appear just as much in equal measure during both times of day. That very much sets them apart from other types of shadow beings. While it's not completely unheard of for other types of shadow entities to show themselves or get caught materializing during the day, it occurs far less often with the types that do not fit in under the header I've assigned to the travelers.

There are times when they are said to be seen in conjunction with another incredibly strange and still unexplained phenomenon that's become much more popular in recent years, and that's the encounters of the vanishing cars. I've seen it quite often lately, someone will write to or otherwise contact me and tell me about how they were driving down some dark and deserted road, usually right at about dusk time, when they see a car come speeding towards them head-on or doing something otherwise and equally as strange. As they look, inside the car where the driver should be there is sometimes no one, almost as if the car is a phantom or from some other time and place where it's perfectly normal for them to be driving and otherwise operating of their own accord and free will. Other times, though, the car will be occupied by one or several shadow entities. These entities seem to want to make the witness think they are in some sort of danger, and in at least eighty percent of the dozens of cases I have come across, right before impact of this impending head-on collision, the car and the entities in it disappear in a fantastic blink and flash of light. It's almost cartoonish the way in which it simply blinks out of existence. There's nothing funny about it, though, at least not in my opinion, as this is yet another terrifying trend that leads me to believe that there is in fact some place, somewhere, where shadow entities of all types, shapes and sizes rule, and they are free to come and go as they please.

There is another possibility here, though, and I would like to mention it just briefly. What if these entities in the disappearing cars aren't travelers but TIME travelers instead? What if, as the witness sees a shadow being driving and others occupying the vehicle, these beings and entities are seeing the witness in the exact same way? What if it's all a part of the "thinning of the veil" that's said to be happening between this world and the others around and possibly connected to it, in this decadent and very modern age? Again I ask, what if we are the ones in these specific scenarios being described, in some alternate universe or dimension somewhere, as shadow beings who blinked out of existence along with their vehicle just as fast as we allege when speaking of our own experiences?

Chapter 13
Bloody Mary, the Old Hag and Doppelgangers

No list of shadow entities would be complete if we didn't at least acknowledge that, though much of the time they are male, there is at least one very well-known female shadow entity. The old hag. Let's discuss what we consider to be an old hag here on this plane and not so much in the supernatural sense of an experience with her. An elderly woman who is most often very unattractive. I always think of a bent-over, haggard, gray-skinned woman with balding but long, straggly and knotted gray hair and a wart on her long and crooked nose. Yes, this is more like the Brothers Grimm version of "witch," but this is just how I picture her. In a supernatural sense, though, the old hag is something much different and much more terrifying.

One victim of this ageless creature said of their terrifying experience with her, "The sleep hag is the dark figure standing over my bed. She is the reason I fear the dark. She is the reason my body wants to run but cannot. She has all the power of the night."

Allegedly, just like with most sleep paralysis encounters, this dark figure wants one thing and one thing only, and that's to suck the life out of the person it is focused on and/or attacking in that moment. That's the legend at least.

There is one such entity who is a part of a very well-known urban legend who I believe is a shadow entity. There is much debate as to who she really is, and because this is supposedly just an urban legend, all you know is what you hear secondhand from someone who knew someone else who told them what the truth might actually be. I have always been too much of a scaredy-cat to play the game Bloody Mary myself. However, upon doing some research into who she could have been in life, I am more apt to believe that she was a very powerful, natural witch who was burned for being one. Where this happened, who knows? I know that in most of the legends I heard, she was from Europe and a queen once who loved to bathe in the blood of her servants and other peasant girls. At least the young and pretty ones. While I agree Mary Bathory was a sick and twisted woman, I do not believe for a second she was a witch and therefore don't even entertain the notion that she may have been powerful enough to cast such a spell as to be able to appear in bedroom and bathroom mirrors all over the world, simply from a summoning.

The more I investigate this phenomenon and the

more real encounters that I come across, the ones I genuinely believe had encounters with this entity, the more I see that they were indeed attacked in the dark by some sort of shadow entity. A female one. Could the female entities be altogether different from the males in this way? Could most of the female shadow apparitions we encounter be spirits of onetime witches who were so callously murdered? This would put them in a league with ghosts and spirits, and I just can't take a hard stance one way or another on this particular topic of debate.

Let's take Bloody Mary, for instance. What is it? What happens? The ritual has changed throughout the centuries, and as far as I can tell, it started out innocently enough with a group of young girls holding a lit candle and walking backwards down the stairs with it in an otherwise darkened home. As they gazed in the mirrors, if they were lucky, they would be able to catch a glimpse of their future husband's face. The divination ritual has since changed many times throughout the ages, and now there is a much simpler one but with a much steeper, and more terrifying, price to be paid than the possible glance at a handsome face. We go into the bathroom at a slumber party, normally in groups of three or more, and we each have a lit candle. Even a tea light will do. We then all look into the mirror and call her name three times. "Bloody Mary, Bloody Mary, Bloody Mary." Our candle then blows out on its own despite the lack of wind or breeze in the room with us. When we look up and into the mirror, there is a demonic face there. Perhaps it is the face of a witch or a hag or even of Medusa herself. You leave the bathroom physically unscathed but emotionally weary from the fear but all the while thinking you somehow just got away with something.

The real curse of Bloody Mary comes later on that night, after the teens, or whoever it was, realize that they didn't actually see anything at all in the mirror and that they were suckers in believing the legend in the first place. However, from that night on, they are doomed to be attacked and haunted in their sleep by a presence. A shadow entity sitting on their chests in the middle of the night, and if it was a man or boys who summoned her, then look out—she becomes like a succubus, and they will never find rest again.

You see, this isn't some tall tale or urban legend I am telling you. I am simply relaying to you what I have experienced during walkthroughs of other people's homes. So many times, their teenagers are being tormented in the night, and only they and I know why. So how is it that the female shadow entities can appear as this urban legend? The fact of the matter is it is a way that we let the devil and evil into our homes, and these beings have a tendency to prey on the more innocent and the weak. That's why it's quite common for black-eyed children to get the invitation they are so desperate for from other children. These teenagers just want a good scare, but after that night, unless they call in someone like me, they won't ever find peace. Many times the parents don't want to admit that this isn't all some elaborately pulled-off trick by their kids on them. I've been there when it finally dawns on all involved that this is, very much so, a life-or-death situation.

The entity, though appearing only in shadow, will, instead of her male counterpart's hat, be wearing a long, flowing gown of some much older fashion. She always has long and flowing hair as well. Her eyes glow a burning, bright red in some cases. I don't believe Bloody Mary was ever more than a mere witch who was crossed, and I believe there is far more than just one, especially given the number of reports and encounters that have come across my desk throughout the course of my short career.

There is a girl named Ekho who sent in an encounter she claims she had with a female shadow entity right after trying to summon Bloody Mary back in 1998. She was thirteen at the time and was at a sleepover with five other girls. They were up watching scary movies and decided to try to "play" the urban legend game. Three of the girls went into the bathroom while one refused to take part and sat on the bed, and the other stood guard at the bedroom door to make sure the brother of the girl whose party it was didn't come in or anything else that would interrupt the "game." The girls went in with their lit candles and said the name the recommended amount of times. Nothing happened, at least not immediately.

The next day all of the girls woke up around six in

the morning right as the sun was starting to shine. They all remembered having the same vivid dream of a woman coming out of the mirror and skulking around the bedroom, stopping to look into the eyes of each girl, one by one. The woman, as she stared into the terrified eyes and as they tried to move their immobilized bodies, would open her mouth as if to scream, but nothing would come out. Her jaw would unhinge unnaturally wide, and she just stood there, leaning over them in either the bed or the sleeping bags they were lying in. Her jaws were massive like those of a serpent about to devour a whole antelope. The image itself is enough to give someone nightmares for the rest of their lives let alone having to experience it for the rest of your time here too!

Let's round this out by briefly mentioning the doppelgangers. This is another well-known entity that I am asking you to throw away all of your preconceived notions on it and try to stay with me as I take you through why I included them in a book about shadow entities and sleep paralysis. I am not saying all doppelgangers are shadow people, but I am saying there have been cases where they behave enough of the same way that I have to at least consider the possibility that they are either connected in some way or that this is just another known entity in which the shadow beings take on its form in order to confuse the victim and keep them from researching too closely into what is actually happening to them. After all, if you have an experience with a doppelganger, you aren't going to immediately start investigating into shadow people and vice versa. It takes a lot of trial and error, time, patience and research to be able to make this connection work, but I am willing to try to bring you down the rabbit hole for a few moments, that is, if you will allow me to.

The word doppelganger is derived from the German words "double goer," and it has had its origins in the paranormal and supernatural world from the very beginning. There are three main theories as to what doppelgangers actually are. I'll sum them up for you. The first is that they are the shadow self of the person encountering them, and though they barely make themselves known, there are always exceptions to this rule, and they usually show themselves when the person is weak and vulnerable for whatever reason. They're said to be harbingers of doom, ill fate and bad luck, and this is something we have already discussed some people think shadow beings in general could be. The second theory is that they are supernatural beings like demons or spirits who appear in order to take over and possess the victim for mysterious and unknown reasons and purposes. A form of possession, if you will. The third theory I am going to mention here is the one that says that doppelgangers are in fact the real, physical manifestation of the victim's spirit who comes and somehow takes form here in the physical world. We are going to discuss the shadow theory because I believe, at least in some cases, a person is actually experiencing a doppelganger and not a shadow person at all, besides that it's the form the thing has chosen to take on, for whatever reasons.

There is a report I came across from a woman in the United States somewhere who claims that she encountered a shadowy doppelganger right after moving into her new home with her new husband. She starts off by explaining that the master bedroom had a gigantic dresser, which stood directly next to a very large, walk-in closet. The woman remembers jumping up one night, seemingly out of a very peaceful sleep, and coming face-to-face with something terrifying standing there next to the dresser, somewhat leaning out from the closet. At first, she thought it was her husband and explained, "One night, I woke up all of a sudden. I was facing the walk-in closet. I saw my husband in the middle of it, his back facing me, just looking around the closet. It's hard to say how I recognized this person as my husband because all I could see was what looked like the back of a head. It was all shadow but it was wearing his clothes. The same clothes he had been wearing before we went to bed that night. I thought it was really strange for him to walk into the closet, since none of his belongings were in there and plus it was in the middle of the night. I propped myself up and asked him what he was doing in my closet and to come back to bed. His face turned slightly, but only just enough for me to see half of his shadowy cheek. I was really exhausted, so I laid back down and fell asleep. I'm not sure how much time had passed, but I woke up again to my husband getting into bed. This time he looked perfectly normal but I was still very confused and I asked him why he had just been in the closet. He told me he didn't know what I was talking about, he just went to the bathroom. We both fell back asleep, and I tried to continue the conversation in the morning. He swore he just went to the bathroom and it took no longer than one minute. He thought I was definitely dreaming, but I know what I saw. That person in the closet was my husband or at least looked 100% like him. I can't think of any logical explanation. Even if my husband had some reason to lie, it doesn't explain why he looked like nothing more than a mere shadow when I first noticed him standing there."

While I'll admit this is the only encounter with a shadow entity where the witness reported that they were not only wearing clothes but were clearly wearing real human clothes that belonged to someone the witness was close to. However, I don't deny that this could have been something altogether different, and that's the most frustrating thing for me when it comes to this topic. It could have literally been anything. I feel though that this entity was caught doing something, I don't pretend to know what, and that it gave her the suggestion to go back to sleep, so she did. It either left immediately or finished up whatever business it had there, and that was that. It wasn't that woman's husband there in the closet that night, but unfortunately that's all I know for an absolute fact, as I couldn't find any follow-up at all from this particular witness and am unsure how this all ended up playing out. Shadow entities are bad enough, but when you add shadow doppelgangers into the mix, you are dealing with a whole different kind of terror. I wonder what experiences she and her husband had after that night.

Chapter 14
Shadow Entities and the Extraterrestrial Connection

In the winter of 1961 in Boston, Massachusetts, a young woman named Sally Salisbury was awoken in the early hours from a very deep sleep. Her eyes opened to the absolutely most horrifying sight one could ever pray to not have to wake up to themselves, a sinister shadow entity looming directly over her, vertically even with her body as she lay there in her bed. Sally claimed that the entity was penetrating her to her very core with feelings of hatred and malevolence. As she went to move, she quickly realized that her body was in a total state of paralysis, but her mind was wide awake and sharp. It was about two or three minutes later that the entity vanished right before her eyes and seemingly into thin air, and she was able to move again.

The next night she had a very interesting and vivid dream where she was abducted by extraterrestrials and taken from her bedroom and aboard their craft. It was here where she remembered having been experimented on. The procedures performed on and done to young Sally were not only intrusive but extremely personal as well, with some of the experiments being done on her private areas. This is where the connection seemingly comes in between shadow entities and extraterrestrials. One often seems to precede or follow the other, and I have always felt they were somehow connected, only with how vague and almost nonexistent the credible and factual information is about both types of entities/creatures, it's basically impossible to either prove it or say how it could be. Call it a hunch based on the hundreds of encounters I've come across where the person was experiencing both abduction phenomenon and shadow entities on a regular basis.

In the village of Barton-Under-Needwood in Staffordshire, England, there was a family called the Morrises. A short time after eleven p.m. on October 4, 1972, the family were driving along when they suddenly saw what appeared to be a small and metallic-looking UFO. The craft was simply hovering there, directly in front of them, in the middle of the road. They were forced to slam on the brakes and make the car come to a screeching halt in order to avoid colliding with this otherworldly ship. The object merely floated there as the family watched in awe and wonder. Within twenty-seconds of stopping the car and beholding this incredible sight, the UFO suddenly and without warning took off at an inhuman and unnaturally high rate of speed and disappeared into the night sky.

So, what does this have to do with shadow entities? Almost immediately after this encounter, the entire family started having some very strange dreams and visions. Namely George Morris, the father, had dreamt he was taken aboard the ship. His wife, Sheila, had vivid and recurring nightmares of, while back at the car on the night they encountered the UFO, being visited by a very creepy and very small humanoid creature that was standing by the family's car. The being was seen as all shadow. Nowadays most of us in this community will recognize that these aren't dreams at all or even visions but are deeply repressed memories of an actual abduction experience. The memory of simply stopping and staring at the craft as it hovered there before them was merely a screen memory.

There is a very large percentage of people who claim to have been abducted by aliens who say that, within a month or two after the abduction, they are haunted by the sight of shadow beings all throughout their home. For many of these people this is their first ever experience with anything supernatural or paranormal. So, on top of having to deal with all that comes with being abducted by extraterrestrials, these people then have to, simultaneously almost, come to terms with the fact that there are now dangerous, malevolent and totally mysterious shadow entities haunting them in the night as well. Could it be, though, that the shadow entities themselves are actually something akin to or are in fact "invisible" extraterrestrials? Perhaps ones involved directly with their abductions or ones who are assigned to watch over and essentially "protect" the human subject? In other words, to care and look out for the extraterrestrials' investment? It stands to reason that even if someone or something is turned invisible, they still keep their own mass about them, right? Is it possible that the only way the human eye is capable of perceiving this mass is in the form of a shadow? This is not to say that every single person who has ever been abducted has then had their lives and homes overrun by shadow people or that people who are infested with shadow entities are that way because they were also abducted at some point. It is happening at a somewhat alarming rate all throughout the world.

This has never been more evident than in the case of twenty-seven-year-old Kelly Cahill and her family, who claim to have been abducted back in August of 1993. Kelly was a housewife and had three children. The Cahills were all in the family car one night on their way to a birthday party for one of Kelly's friend's daughters. The family were driving between Belgrave and Fountain Gate in Victoria, Australia. It was seven at night and it had just gotten fully dark outside. They were driving past the Dandenong Mountain Range, which was right near the housing estate where the party was being held in Melbourne. It was a quiet and suburban area, and everything was nice and peaceful, even with a car full of excited children. The road was dark and very isolated with few other cars around. This is why it stood out so much to Kelly that there was a vehicle with a man and woman in it that was pulled over on the side of the road, seemingly for no reason.

Kelly was in the passenger seat, with her husband doing the driving, and she started to doze off as she watched the trees outside the window pass her by. Before she could fully fall asleep though, and as the area and landscape became more and more mountainous with each mile passed, Kelly was becoming very, almost unnaturally, relaxed. However, she saw something in the sky that would jolt her awake and change the lives of her and her family forever. There was suddenly what looked to be "an orange string of lights" in the sky. She turned to her husband wide eyed and somewhat shocked and told him she had just seen a UFO. Kelly's husband laughed and thought it was absolutely adorable that his wife was mistaking a helicopter for an alien craft. He was driving though, and it's doubtful he really was able to get a good look at the lights because of that.

Before long, they had arrived at the party, and the evening passed by fairly normally, with both Kelly and her husband having already forgotten about the strange orange lights in the sky. As they drove home, though, they saw the lights once again, and Kelly was sure they were the same ones she had seen before.

They were taking the same route home as they had taken there in the first place, and it seemed as though the lights hadn't moved very far in the few hours since they had passed by this spot last.

Kelly would talk a lot about what she had experienced that night and she told one interviewer, whose name was Rob Tilley, this about what had taken place: "Anyway, we were driving back down the road in the same stretch. Both of us, just me and my husband... we both saw this ring, mind you... in front of us, hovering above the road. It was just something sitting there... I couldn't tell what it was. We were at first far away, but as you got closer to it was sort of... well, it wasn't like the orange light in the field. It was a round shape with some sort of glass around, or what looked like windows and lights around the bottom. Because it was dark, you couldn't really tell at first. But as we got closer and closer, there was no noise or anything. Even my husband's going. 'You're right! That's something. That's very, very strange.' And I swear we saw people in there, and then just as I said to him, 'I swear there's people in there,' it just shot off to the left as fast as it could go. I mean it just disappeared. Within a split second it had gone. We kept driving and about a kilometer ahead, all of a sudden, there's this really, really bright light in front of us, and I've got my hand up, up above my brow, to look out the window, because it's that bright, but I can't see anything. I said to [my husband], 'What are you going to do?' He said, 'I'm going to keep driving.'

From there, that is the last we remembered until... I knew I was going to see a UFO, you know, I just knew, because of what we had seen, I'd seen it twice in one night and he had seen it once... and the adrenaline is pumping, the heart is thumping, I'm so excited. All of a sudden I'm sitting in the car, and I'm saying to my husband, 'What happened?' And he says to me, 'I don't know. We must have gone around a corner or something.'"

The couple suddenly felt a sense of strangeness that crept over them like a blanket of fog was enveloping their minds. They had no idea why they were feeling so out of sorts, but they couldn't shake the feeling, and they were both very uncomfortable. Although there seemed to be no sign of where it was coming from, there was a smell similar to vomit pervading the family car as well. The couple tried to remain calm for the sake of the children, but they began to discuss this grim and overwhelming feeling of doom with one another. It seems, though, this was the last thing they should have done because, according to Kelly, as they continued driving home from the party, they passed a strange and seemingly supernatural figure along the side of the road. Kelly described it as "tall and dark" and admitted that she didn't think that it was human.

Once the family got home, they realized an hour of time was completely missing from both of their minds. The time frame for how long it took to get from the party to home wasn't adding up, and neither of them could remember what had gone down during that missing hour. It was once they were home that Kelly also discovered a very strange marking on her body that she obviously knew wasn't there before they had left the house that day and that she couldn't explain. It was a bizarre triangular marking, and it was located right above her navel, and directly on top of it was a random and brand-new scar. As confused as they all were, they tried to put the whole bizarre experience behind them and move on with their lives.

However, in the weeks to come, Kelly started menstruating erratically and completely off of her cycle. Both she and her husband were experiencing severe abdominal pain, headaches, nausea, and an extreme feeling of tiredness and fatigue too. Kelly became so sick she was barely able to walk on her own, and eventually her husband had to rush her to the nearest hospital. The doctors then told the couple that Kelly had some sort of infection in her womb.

While all of this was going on, Kelly started to have these strange daytime dreams where she would remember fragments, just bits and pieces, of what had happened to her and her family on the night of August 8 while driving back from that party at her friend's house. She didn't realize that that's what they were though, at least not at first. She remembered first going towards and stepping into the brightest light she had ever seen in her life. In that blinding light, though, she remembered seeing all kinds of strange shadow beings.

One day when she and her husband drove past the exact same spot where all of this had originally taken place, a sense of overwhelming terror and dread came over Kelly. She said, "On the way home from bingo that night, we went along the same road, and as we passed a certain spot, I just got this incredible feeling of terror go through me, I mean absolute terror. All of a sudden I just started remembering, and by the next morning I had remembered just about everything that happened, except there's still missing time that I can't. What we had actually done, we had driven into the light, but the road curved, and the light we had thought was in front of us was actually to our right-hand side. It was in the field, and it was massive... the 'size of a house' or perhaps close to 50 meters. So it was very big. Why I knew it was very big was because we could have driven for five minutes. The road sort of wound around this part. You could have driven for five minutes and not had it out of your sight the whole time."

She and her husband both remembered pulling over to the side of the road and, after parking, getting out of the car to approach and get a better look at this strange light. The car that she had originally remembered with the man and woman in it now held a different and perhaps more significant memory to her. She said she recalled another car, also pulled over to the side of the road and having three people who exited the vehicle and started walking off into the fields surrounding them.

Kelly then turned her attention from the other people to the now very visible unidentified spacecraft right in front of her. This is when she noticed there was an unusually tall and very dark black figure who stood at seven feet tall or more. This entity had terrifying eyes, which Kelly described as, "burning red, like... fluorescent stop lights, I suppose, that sort of real burning red." Kelly was beside herself with fear and dread. The entity was now approaching her and her husband. She said of what happened next, "All of a sudden, I started screaming out to my husband... Now this has really got me baffled because of the fact that a human being doesn't know this, so I don't even know how I came out with this, but I started saying, 'They've got no souls.' And then I started screaming, 'THEY'VE GOT NO SOULS!' Then all of a sudden there were heaps of them in the field, not just one, a whole heap of them, and they started coming towards us... faster than a man could run, and they were gliding off the ground. They got halfway across the field. They split up. Some of them went towards the other people [two or three, Kelly thought]. and some of them [the rest] came towards us. I was hysterically terrified... I had never felt terror like that. Not even in my worst nightmares had I experienced terror like that. The next thing I know, I felt this oomph! in my stomach, right across here like I was winded, but I was thrown right back, and I was on my back on the ground. I sat up, with my head between my knees. Here, I'm trying to stay conscious. I couldn't see. My eyes... It was all black."

As the creatures approached, they continuously bombarded her with telepathic messages reiterating and possibly trying to reassure her in order to keep her calm, that they "meant no harm." Kelly was barely aware of her husband, who stood very silently beside her the whole time. It was almost like he was disappearing into the craziness of the whole ordeal, and she had to keep grabbing his arm to remind herself she wasn't alone and that this was all actually happening for real. Kelly felt that, regardless of the constant reassurances as to the contrary, that every single one of these strange beings was pure, soulless evil. Finally, her anger bubbled up and seemed to overtake even her fear. It was raw and pure, unadulterated rage at these evil beings who were now fast approaching Kelly and her husband. Kelly cussed and shouted at the beings. She threatened them and told them to go away and leave her and her family alone. However, as far as Kelly's memory recalled it, at that moment, the next thing she remembered was being back in her car and feeling as though something was "off."

In the following weeks after remembering all that she had, Kelly started to have more vivid dreams, dreams she was sure weren't dreams at all but fractions of wiped memory from the night she and her family were abducted by the aliens. Kelly talked about these dreams and said, "When after I did remember it,

I had another dream, and these dreams seemed very physical. I know I'm dreaming, and I've got to wake up out of them... In this particular one, I felt as if my legs were being pulled off the bed, and it was like I was paralyzed from my waist down, and my legs were being pulled over to the side; yet I could almost use the top of my body. Then I'm grabbing a pillow, trying to hit my husband, to wake him up... I'm fighting this. I'm not going to let this thing drag me off the bed by my legs. Then I woke up and saw it standing there again! This time the hood covered the eyes, and it didn't scare me... I was still terrified, but it didn't scare me quite as much, because each time it scared me, it was that same power like I felt out in the field that night."

Throughout this entire ordeal, Kelly's husband wasn't able to remember anything and had no clue what she was talking about when she tried, desperately I'm sure, to discuss it with him. Kelly would eventually contact a reporter in Sydney, Australia, named Bill Chalker, who worked for the UFO Investigation Center. Bill launched a very in-depth and thorough investigation into Kelly and her claims. He also called in the group PRA or "Paranormal Research Australia" to help assist him with his investigation. These investigators did an amazing job and were even able to track down not only the couple who Kelly originally saw on the side of the road on the way to the party, but also the three individuals who she said were walking towards the field and the ship at the same time she and her husband were. All of these people, five of them in total, had the exact same triangular mark in the exact same spot as Kelly did. Bill Chalker and his team were able to somewhat prove at least that something unusual had happened that night. In the exact spot where Kelly had said the ship had landed and the beings approached her and the others, they found several chemical and magnetic anomalies, strange and unexplained markings all throughout the field and an unusually high radiation reading.

Kelly Cahill would become a sort of local celebrity, at least for a little while, when this whole abduction experience hit the local news. She appeared at UFO conferences, on television shows about the paranormal and otherworldly, in order to educate others and talk about her experience. She even went on to write a book about it in 1997 titled, *Encounter*. Over the years more and more detail would be added to the retelling of her experience. She claims she was simply remembering more but there are skeptics, as there always are, who claim she may be adding more and more as the years go by to try to keep her story relevant—and making money. Some of the things she has added as time passed by were she and her family being harassed by an unmarked, black helicopter immediately following the experience. She also said she had formed some sort of telepathic and psychic connection to the aliens who had abducted her that night, and they continuously warned her of their plan to invade and take over planet Earth.

Despite the many people who feel Kelly is just trying to keep herself in the spotlight and make money off of her alleged encounter, more often than not she is seen as a reliable and honest witness. She is well respected in the ufology community as well. We must keep in mind when deciding if we believe this almost absurd and fantastical encounter story that Kelly had no prior history of hallucinations or mental illness of any kind. She really had no reason at all to lie about any of it, and she had no prior connection to or interest in the field of ufology. Her neighbors and friends consistently described her as honorable, honest and kind. The Cahill case is an extremely significant one in the field of ufology. Her impeccable and honest reputation added to the facts I just stated above, and the presence of all of the physical evidence the investigators found to back up her claims makes her encounter story stand out as honest and having really happened.

Bill Chalker said of this particular case, "Here we have a striking situation. Two groups of persons unknown to each other have witnessed the same UFO encounter and entities. They also experienced missing time, and each group has been available to competent investigators. Independent witnesses have provided information which enables cross-checking and correlations to reveal a remarkable amount of similar information. The result is a compelling case for the reality of the strange events described. The ontological status of the events is further strengthened by a range of apparently related physical traces, including ground traces, a magnetic anomaly, and effects on some of the witnesses."

While Kelly's case is certainly baffling and quite unbelievable, it's a hard one to really figure out and dig too deep into. Though the Phenomena Research Australia, despite swearing they collected physical evidence as proof the encounter had actually happened, these documents with the data and evidence collected have never been released to the public. The other witnesses are only considered "alleged" due to the fact that they have never been revealed and remain completely anonymous in all of this. Also, the name Kelly Cahill itself is a pseudonym, so at the end of the day we don't even know who this person really is, and neither she nor any of the other supposed witnesses, including her husband, who still can't remember a single bit of what allegedly happened that night, have ever been interviewed by any outside or mainstream source regarding this issue or anything else for that matter. This leaves one of Australia's most infamous UFO and abduction cases shrouded in a thick fog of mystery and doubt.

Almost all shadow entity encounters, when we are also dealing with an abduction experience, are related in some way to what we have come to know in this day and age as "the alien grays." This was almost certainly the case in the Cahill encounter. Could it be that these seemingly altered states of consciousness are the reason that these entities and beings can only be viewed as shadow?

I also think of the reptilians when considering the connection with shadow entities and extraterrestrials. This is mainly due to the fact that all of the ancient legends and myths state that the reptilian race of extraterrestrials needs to continuously drink human blood in order to maintain their human forms. When they attack people in order to obtain this blood from them, they are known to let their disguise slip for just a second or two sometimes. The disguise they choose is one of simple shadow, but every once in a while the witness will see the scales and reptilian's real and true form, and that's when the eyes are revealed. Glowing, red and full of evil and fire, the reptilian emits more of a sense of evil and malevolence than any other form of extraterrestrial I've come to know anything about. This is another way of feeding, mind you. While most shadow entities and extraterrestrials seem to only be after our fear and pain, the reptilians (and more than likely many others as well whom we just aren't aware of yet) will possibly let their shadow disguise slip for that moment or two so that they can also energetically feed. The cuts, scrapes and scratches many people report waking up with after having had a particularly violent interaction with a shadow entity in the night could be how the reptilians get the blood out of us. This is all just my own speculation on the subject, of course, but I would stake a large wager that I am, at least partly, correct in these assumptions.

Chapter 15
The Tricksters

The shadow being I find myself being confronted with the most in the past twenty years or so is one I like to call "the Trickster." Many people will use the term "trickster" to identify one otherworldly entity or another, but keep in mind these are my own personal labels for these entities, so they may be a bit different here than what you are used to. I figured this out after one quick search for "trickster shadow people." The results were all over the place with almost nothing about this almost always Native American spirit. Tricksters are responsible for about seventy-five percent of all shadow entity phenomena I've been called on to investigate in the last few years. Approximately ninety-eight percent of the time, in these cases, the trickster is associated with some old and possibly even ancient Native American tribe.

Each tribe has a different mythology about the trickster entity, but some of the basics remain the same almost throughout. The trickster is very inconsistent in its behavior and appearance. It could appear in shadow most days but sometimes switch it up and appear as an extraterrestrial or a wild animal. The reason I, and a few others, call these specific entities by this name is because they play tricks on people. These aren't little innocent and childish pranks, though; these are evil, cruel and downright dangerous things these smaller entities do to the humans and domestic pets in their environment. These entities stand at less than three feet tall most of the time, and they are master shapeshifters. They love to shift into many frightening and bizarre things, even while still maintaining their shadow appearance. Tricksters act spontaneously, though I feel, in most cases, that they are perfectly capable of rational and reasonable thought. They simply choose not to employ it. Able to pull off flawless impersonations of human beings, other than the lack of speech, they are much of the time the entity behind the so-called "doppelganger" phenomenon.

I would like to give you all a personal example of a time very recently when I came upon a couple of tricksters. On Wednesday nights I go live on my YouTube channel and read one oracle card for anyone and everyone who comes in to receive one. It is a random card, chosen from a random deck, and ends up being the person's weekly reading. I do this for anywhere from three to four hours depending on the crowd, and I've built up the loveliest community around myself and my Wednesday nights. I have a friend who comes in and cohosts the stream with me. His name is Steven, and he takes the list down of the people who come in, in the order they arrive, and then reads the list off as I read for everyone. The people who come into this stream and my subscribers in general are almost all psychically sensitive in some way. They're almost all empaths, and almost all of them have some sort of gift or another.

One night it was just like any other night where I was reading and conversing with Steven and the chat when all of a sudden, I looked up and saw behind Steven three trickster beings walking right out of his wall. What I saw was three very short figures; all of them looked like little kids wearing those old ghost costumes. The ones where the parent would cut holes in the eyes of a sheet and put it on their kid. However, these were all black, not white. It was a rather silly sight, and my first thought was to chuckle, if I'm being honest. I caught them after they had already materialized and couldn't be one hundred percent sure that they didn't come in through the window right behind him.

I said to him, "There are tricksters in your room with you." He said he was aware of their energy and for us not to worry about anything. However, by the end of the stream Steven was silently praying and had somehow ended up with burn marks on the backs of his hands and bruises all over his wrists. These things simply appeared as we all sat there and watched.

Finally, I ended the stream and did what I normally do when I need to connect with someone's energy who is far away from me but whom I need to help. Steven lives in Ohio, and I live in New Jersey, so we are fairly far away from each other to say the least.

Anyway, I connected with the entities and found that they came floating in through the window. I realized almost immediately that only two of these entities were actually tricksters, and the other one was some sort of extraterrestrial. I tried to see what this alien actually looked like, but it kept showing me ET from the actual movie. I couldn't break through its facade. However, when I asked it why it was mimicking the tricksters, it explained that it thought they were interesting and therefore took on the shape that they had taken on, which was the black sheet-looking things I had seen. The tricksters were there, though, and I was more concerned with them.

Steven told me not to worry, but the next morning he had marks around his wrists as though he had been handcuffed, and things all around his bedroom had been obviously moved. He had fragmented memories of being abducted and the other people in his home, who were normally very quiet and soft spoken, had suddenly become aggressive and ornery towards him. This was a problem of the worst kind.

Tricksters do things like trip people down the steps when they're holding an infant or small child. They try to convince small children to bite into live electrical wires or to play with the oven when their parents aren't watching. Once they invade your home, you most likely will be infested with them and tormented until you move. There is no known way to get rid of them except for identifying which tribe they come from and calling the shaman from that tribe and having them come in to remove the entities. However, depending on so many different things like whether or not the people living in the home have abilities of their own and how long the entities have been there, and so much more, they almost never are able to completely rid a space of these things. Once you move though, they almost never follow you. Most people, after dealing with these entities for just a short period of time, are so desperate to be rid of them they decide to take the risk and move, doing so purely out of faith alone and not knowing for sure if the entities will follow them and when.

As for Steven, I sent him what I call a "spiritual helper" box, designed for his specific problem, and he was able to get them at least out of his house and off his property. They still linger, though, and it's only a matter of time before they break through the barriers. He will most likely have to put the same barriers up, along his entire property and in his home, every three months for the rest of his life.

Putting spiritual barriers up around your home is always a gamble. I know so many people believe in this, and if it puts you at ease, then by all means do it. I have seen far too many cases where, mainly when the person lives nearby to some dense wooded areas, the barricades actually lure in other, usually much more evil and deadly entities. These beings take the barricades and protective measures as a challenge, and it is somewhat of an accidental lure for them from the woods to your property and home. Some people believe these tiny shadow entities are actually the spirits and lost souls of children who died outside a state of grace and who are doomed to roam for all of eternity between the worlds of the living and the dead.

One case of a somewhat benign trickster shadow being came to me from a woman named Jessie from Nebraska. Jessie said that she had bought her first home two years earlier, and everything was a dream, until suddenly it wasn't. Seemingly out of nowhere, about two years after she had moved in, she began to experience very strange phenomena in her home. It started off rather benignly with things being moved around and found in very odd places. Her car keys wouldn't be where she had left them hanging on the hook by the door and would eventually be found in the sugar bowl in the kitchen. Her television remotes would turn up, after days of being lost, sitting in plain sight on the coffee table in the living room. At first, she thought she was losing her mind, but things didn't stay so innocent for long. It was a slow progression, though, and aside from the constantly misplaced objects, there eventually started to be odd and seemingly random things happening around the house that no one could explain away. Lights would suddenly burst and explode for no reason, the toilets would flush over and over again when there was nobody even near the bathroom, and objects like pots and pans would fly around the rooms, seemingly aimed at whoever was closest to them at the time. It was getting progressively dangerous, as is usually the case with these devilish entities.

One night Jessie lay down in her bed to go to sleep. She said she had just started to really doze off when a sound coming from her closet jolted her up out of bed and snapped her out of her sleepiness almost immediately. It sounded like someone was knocking on her closet door, from the inside. She listened for a minute or two, but after hearing nothing at all, she decided it must have been her imagination or a trick of the mind from being in that semi-sleep state where everything is fuzzy, and nothing quite makes sense. As soon as she lay back down and closed her eyes again, she heard the knocking again, coming from the inside of the closet. Once again, she sat up to listen better, and once again heard nothing out of the ordinary, from the closet or otherwise.

I'll let her explain what happened next, "I was lying there and minutes went by without another sound. I was starting to think I had imagined it after all or that it was just the house settling (it's a really old house), but then I saw something up by the ceiling at the closet door. It looked like a very deep, black shadow, but there was nothing to cast it, and it did not seem like a normal shadow to me. I sort of blinked a few times and stared at it, and then it moved! It sort of scurried across the ceiling all the way to the other side of the room to a pool of shadow in the corner of the ceiling. It really freaked me out because it looked like a really big spider, complete with spindly legs, only much bigger than anything that should have been there, around the size of a cat. This was when I got out of bed and picked up a hanger that had been lying on the floor. I still had this feeling that there was a big ass spider up there, even though I sensed on some level that this was impossible, and so I crept closer to that shadow on the ceiling thinking I would poke it with the hanger if I saw it, but I could now see there was nothing there. I went back to the bed and thought I was losing my mind and then the same skittering shadow spider thing scrambled down the wall from the exact same spot I had just looked at, and hurried across the floor to the closet door and vanished. There were two loud raps from inside the closet and then it was gone. I didn't sleep that night, I can tell you. The next morning I checked the closet and it was exactly as it always was. I can't explain it at all."

After this incident, all of the other members of Jessie's household started having the same experience. They would see a black shadow creeping around that when they were able to get a good look, they would see what looked to be a giant spider. This is especially significant because of the fact that, though the tricksters nowadays prefer to take on the form of smaller, humanoid shadow beings, this wasn't always the case, and there is a widely known legend throughout and across many Native American cultures that speaks of such a horrific being. Mainly the Lakota, Dakota and Nakota Sioux tribes have a being like this. Its name is Iktomi. The name literally means "spider," and in English he or it is sometimes referred to as "Spiderman" or simply "Spider." Though the entity usually appears as its namesake, in the Sioux legends specifically this entity is depicted as a human man.

Like so many other Plains Indians trickster entities, this one is especially crude. He behaves or influences others to engage in the most socially unacceptable behavior possible and is a very negative and malevolent presence to be around, especially for children. I bring up this next encounter specifically because it seems to be happening at a much higher rate now, off of the reservations and in mainstream society—for lack of a better way of putting it. You don't have to be Native American or have Native blood to have encounters with these shadow spider beings.

A twenty-seven-year-old man wrote to me recently and explained something was happening to him that hadn't happened in about ten years. Something otherworldly that he was sure he had escaped when he left his childhood home, the place where the visions, encounters and overall torment had begun for him when he was only four years old. This man, whom I will call Adam for the sake of anonymity, said that ever since he was a small child, he believed there were "people" whom he could only see as shadow, who would come into his bedroom at night and seemed to only want to watch him sleep. Sometimes, though, they would grab at him, and despite him waking up with unexplained bruises in the shape of fingers or hands, his mother and father would brush it off as the wild and overactive imagination of a little kid. The doctors all said the same thing, concluding Adam was simply, "a restless sleeper" and that nothing was wrong with him, physically or mentally, except for the aforementioned overactive imagination. The poor little kid simply learned to live with the fear and terror that accompanies these nighttime visits and tried as best he could to move on with his life and be a "normal" little boy.

However, as he got older, starting at around the age of ten or so, Adam says things took a very drastic change for the worse when he started seeing something even more strange and terrifying than the original shadow people. The beings wouldn't be there every single night anymore, but when they were, they had company with them. I chose Adam's encounter because he has a very interesting theory about it all. He says that he saw spiders crawling all over himself and his bedroom walls. The spider things seemed to be coming directly from and out of the humanoid shadows he had become so accustomed to. Adam was terrified and would scream at the top of his lungs every time this would happen, which at its most heightened, was several times a week or more. His parents were extremely concerned because they would run into the room and turn the lights on immediately, and Adam explained that as soon as the light would hit these creatures, they would disappear as if they hadn't actually been there at all. He would have small, fanged bite marks all over his body, which did seem to be spider bites. However, the number he had on him at any given time made it seem impossible that that's what this could have actually been. In other words, his parents and doctors didn't believe it was possible for someone to have been bitten so many times by a single spider and surmised that if there were a nest of them somewhere, then surely, they would have been found already.

As the spiders became more and more in their numbers each night, the shadow entities became bolder. They wouldn't only stand over him and sometimes grab his wrists anymore. Now they would sit on his bed or lean into him, their faces right in front of his, and it was terrifying. There was no help or hope in sight for Adam because nobody could understand what was going on, and it was just easier to pretend it was something completely ordinary that they just hadn't figured out yet.

Adam says that he still sees both the humanoid shadow entities and the trickster spiders to this day but has since found ways to protect himself from them, for the most part. He said something interesting while explaining his experiences to me, and that's that he sees "what people perceive to be spiders." This reminded me of something else I picked up along my life of physical mediumship, and that is most human beings' fear of spiders in general. I understand not every single person under the sun is terrified or even a little afraid of spiders, but it is a very common fear. There is a planet somewhere in the galaxy, and I don't pretend to know or understand where, that is inhabited by giant spiders. They are malicious, violent and love to go to war. Some people, or so I've come to understand, with unreasonable fears of spiders, once lived on planets that these beings had overtaken. I wholeheartedly and truly believe this is the case, knowing what I know about reincarnation, otherworldly entities and Spirit. These are cell memories left over from other lives where these spiders invaded whatever planet we were safely living on up until that point.

Also, though most people don't believe they're real, I do swear that at least a few of those random YouTube videos depicting giant spiders that are climbing over houses and crawling over gigantic trees are very real. Why were the shadow spiders seeming to come from the shadow humanoids in Adam's case? I'm sure I don't know, but I do find that when it comes to trickster shadows and children, they will almost always go right for the heart of the child, meaning what it fears the most. This is a common childhood fear. The entities tormented him all night long for years and still make an appearance from time to time. There are plenty of Native American Trickster shadow entities other than the ones who take on the form of the spider, but for most of them, for one reason or another I'm sure I don't yet know, they always go back to the spider image. It's almost like that is their true image and the small humanoids and other animals whose images they take on are the real facade. There is so much more to the legends of why this particular entity's real form is that of a spider and how it all came to be, but to put it all here would be much too much, and I encourage you, as always, to do your own research into these things if they interest you.

Chapter 16
A Personal Experience

For as far back as I can remember, shadow people have been a part of my life. My earliest memories of having convulsions and seizures either randomly or due to extremely high fevers also include these entities. These are my first memories of them. I was six years old and lying on the couch after a particularly bad convulsion with a fever that should've left me rendered unconscious or dead at almost 104 degrees Fahrenheit. I would hallucinate because of it, and I remember so vividly as I lay there on the couch, talking nonsense to my dad, who was trying to cool me down with ice and a cold rag, (it was the '80s, so I guess you didn't have to take your children to the hospital if you didn't want to) strange and scary figures stepped into the room. Even at that age I knew the difference between what I was hallucinating and what was real, at least after the fact.

These figures seemed to step right out of the wall. It was nighttime and dark in the room, as the light would only make me hotter and sicker. There was a really tall one, a male as best I can tell simply by his form and, honestly, my intuition. He was wearing a hat and had glowing red eyes. Though he had no facial features and there was no expression to be seen, I somehow knew he had an evil grin. To his left was a much shorter figure, it didn't look like a person but had the shadowy outline of an animal. Nothing I had ever seen before or since, but it was definitely a "pet" or "minion" of the taller man with the hat. It was snarling.

Apparently, all of this, the sights and sounds, were only visible and audible to me, as my dad, though seeing the terror in my eyes, acknowledged it only to tell me to close my eyes and try to sleep and that it would all be ok in the morning. My Irish Catholic father, bless his heart, still to this day refuses to accept my psychic abilities and believes anything having to do with Spirit, whether good or bad, is evil and "mumbo jumbo."

Anyways, back to the shadow entities. The person to the left of the hat man was a female. Again, she had no particular or specific form, but I just knew from the energy she gave off she was a woman, or at least that's what she was projecting to me. I don't technically think any shadow people are male or female because those are human labels, and none of them are human, nor have they ever been. All three of these figures stepped right out of the wall, out of the shadows and darkness of the night, and all three were lusting after my sickness. They wanted to feed off of my weakness and pain, but even more than that, they wanted to taste my terror. They stayed where they were, just staring at me. The animal thing growling and snorting. Making gross sounds that somehow made me want to puke even more. These things were physically and psychically affecting me.

My dad finally decided my fever had gone down enough and asked if I wanted to stay on the couch or sleep in his room. I chose his room, hoping these beings wouldn't be able to get to me if my dad was there. It seems I was right, too, as once he picked me up and carried me out of the living room, I looked back, and all three had slipped once more into the shadows of the room. I went to sleep and woke up the next day feeling physically much better but an emotional wreck, as I somehow just knew what I had seen the night before hadn't been the figment of the high fever but very real. I hoped and prayed I wouldn't encounter them again, but those prayers, unfortunately, weren't answered.

These three figures have shown up throughout my life, since that first night so long ago in 1989, so many times now that I've lost count. They don't only show up when I'm sick anymore either, as it was just a month later that I saw them again. I was playing in my room with my dolls when suddenly I felt all of the hairs on my body stand up and a cold chill enter the room. Now, as a psychically gifted child, I immediately knew this feeling, only at that point in time I related it to Spirit. I thought I was about to have a visitation from the other side. In a way I was right, I guess, but it wasn't the kind I had come to know and was expecting. I looked up from my dolls into my dimly lit room, and there the three entities were again, standing in the corner by my bedroom closet. Only one of them had eyes that I could see. The "pet" thing and the woman were simply silhouettes, and for me, that was terrifying enough.

I asked them what they wanted, but of course I got no answer. Not out loud anyway. I didn't realize until I was much older and much more advanced with my abilities that I had received an answer that night and always received one whenever I would ask them things. You see, the response was telepathic. In my head so as to confuse me and make me think these thoughts were my own. I suddenly thought, "Why don't I go to bed? It's nighttime, after all, and I'm so very tired." I lay down and fell fast asleep, even with these entities standing there and watching me. That in and of itself was strange enough. I would wake up constantly in a state of what we now call "sleep paralysis." Feeling as though I couldn't speak or move or scream out for my dad. I couldn't breathe most of the time, and it was absolutely terrifying. I would try to fight, but of course it was in vain. I could see it was the woman who would hold me down while the man stood next to the bed and leaned over me, peering into my eyes and not letting me shut them. The pet would be next to me on my bed as if it were my own domestic animal, and I could feel its foul breath on my face. I couldn't turn away. I was completely helpless and at their mercy. I could hear their thoughts though. Eventually I would just pass back out.

Things like this would happen a lot to me and eventually I became introverted and weird. I couldn't tell anyone what was happening. My dad would never believe me, and the other kids would make fun of me. Fast forward to when I was about twenty-two years old and living on my own. By this time I had had hundreds of nights like the one I just described, but this is when I finally started researching what exactly I was dealing with. There wasn't much of a World Wide Web in 2002. It was all in its infancy. I would go to the library and look the old-fashioned way but still didn't find much help. It was at this point when I decided to ask my spirit guides to help me or at least explain what these things are and what they want. I was told I'm not allowed to know what they are, only that they come from a place that is "other," but that I should always remember that telepathy can go both ways. I decided to put this thought into action.

The next time they visited, I asked them what they wanted using my mind. This, of course, wasn't while I was under any kind of attack. They didn't just come for that. They came just to lurk and stare and strike the fear of God into me, or so it seemed. By this time I had three children and noticed when I was pregnant, each time I received more visits than normal and was starting to wonder if my kids could see them as well.

Especially my oldest. It turns out, he could. That's another story altogether though. Maybe for another time.

I would sit and have conversations with these beings. I would ask questions, and they would usually answer. Is it so strange that after all of this, I started to consider these shadow entities, the dead I communicated with on a regular basis, and my guides my only friends? They told me, over time of course, that they were from another place and time. They explained that they were there for my energy. I asked them why they seemed so evil, and they said it's only because they would be considered "evil" as humans perceive evil to be but that they really weren't and that I was simply helping them out. They explained that the shadow is the only form they are able to take on while in this realm or on this planet. Once I started having these long conversations with them, I found they were attacking me on a significantly less regular basis. I'll spare you the repetitive and somewhat monotonous details of all of their visits from this point until now and tell you about my more recent experiences.

You see, it's 2022 as I sit and write this, and I still get monthly visits from these same three entities. The only time I went more than a month without a visit was when, in 2016, I was baptized Christian and reborn. I also saw a healer that same week who told me to call out in the name of the Lord when I experienced these "sleep paralysis episodes," and they would be forced to leave me alone and stop. It actually works. I somehow summon the inner strength to say the Lord's prayer, even if I can just recite it in my head, and they back off. They still come and lurk.

They like to lurk over my four-year-old son. He is also highly sensitive but somehow doesn't seem to see these particular entities. Makes sense to me, as they explained they were "assigned to" me and not for others to witness. I no longer engage them, and in fact, I pretend most of the time like they aren't there. But I see them. When I am reading oracle cards for friends and clients. When I'm meditating or channeling. When I wake up in the middle of the night to get a glass of water. I walk right past them as though they aren't there. It's been about thirty-two years now of experiencing these shadow beings, and I still have no idea if anything they told me is true or not. I am very much of the opinion that they are demonic in nature, possibly Djinn, and that the "pet" is in fact some sort of hellhound. They are definitely lower vibrational. I'm hoping one day to write a book to let the world know about my encounters and conversations with these beings who claim to only come from a place that is "other."

I am much stronger in my faith these days and have fully embraced my psychic self. I have seen other shadow entities, or "shadow people" as they're more commonly called. In fact, I see at least one almost every single day. A lot of the time, though, these visitations aren't really for me, and I'll see one stalking the perimeter of my home or that of one of my neighbors. I'll see them loitering around the grocery store, both inside and out. They come and they go, and I go on pretending as though I don't see them. I put up protection charms and little spells to keep all evil and negative entities and energies away from me and my family, and it definitely works. Somehow though, these shadow beings are still able to come and go as they please, and they are connected to me and not the property my house is on or anyone else here. Nobody else sees them, but I wonder sometimes if they have influence over other people who come to my house. Especially over my husband, who lives in it, as the significant and negative changes in his behavior and attitude since I met him are alarming. I am currently working on finding out more about that.

I could go on and on, and in fact, I think one day I will, in a book or series of them regarding these three whom I call "the family" and all of the terror they've provided throughout my life. The main thing one could take away here is that, whether religious or spiritual or not, the Lord's prayer or any prayer to Him will almost always make them stop their physical and psychic attacks, in the moment at least. It's very rare that someone I suggested this to comes back and says it didn't work. It happens, but it's highly unusual when it does.

I hope one day I will wake up and the heaviness in my soul that these beings seem to be the cause of is lifted and I'll immediately know they're no longer with me. I'm not so sure at this point though if that will be a huge comfort or a major disappointment, as I still don't know much about them. They know everything about me, and at times have even alerted me to things about to happen to help me to avoid them. This is what evil does though. It throws you a bone every once in a while, so it can say, "Look at how helpful I am. You should definitely trust me." Don't do it, folks! I know many people have told me that they had infestations of shadow people and were able to get rid of them by doing this or trying that. That's awesome! It won't work for me though. These things are attached to me and have been since as long as I can remember. Like, a part of my extended family. I would much rather deal with spirits and the dead— even the ones who come to me looking grisly and horrific. I can easily interpret their intentions. That's what is so fascinating yet terrifying for me; the fact that I have literally no clue or idea what these things actually are, where they come from, or what their purpose is. I'll have more for you all as my research continues.

Chapter 17
The Static Man

The Static Man or Static Entity is another entity that we know almost nothing about. In fact, we know even less about this one than about the shadow beings in general, and by a lot too. I bring these entities to you in this book because they remind me so much of shadow entities, and in fact, I believe that's exactly what they are. Only, instead of appearing as an all-black, dark shadow, they appear as white shadow or "TV fuzz." In my opinion, this just goes to show that they are made of pure energy. When it starts to get low, they must come out and feed, and here is yet another entity that almost solely focuses on our most innocent, weak and vulnerable, our children. Sure, there are more than a few supernatural and/or paranormal beings that are witnessed solely by children and no one else for one reason or another depending on the entity.

Static entities are seemingly made of flickering white noise or static, and many children have reported having strange and oftentimes terrifying experiences with them. I became aware of this phenomenon some time ago but completely forgot about it with all of my other research and just who I am as a human being in getting distracted and moving on to something else halfway through my research. These beings seem to flicker in and out and aren't as seemingly solid as their dark cousins. I have a feeling that we only see them when they are described as "flickering" because they are low on energy and hungry. So far, I can't categorize or classify them, but I have no problem with grouping them in as a relative to shadow entities. Possibly I could say they're kind of humanoid and almost exclusively seen by children.

Sometimes they confuse, and most times they strike fear in the hearts of whoever lays eyes on them. This is not just because they're paranormal, mind you; they may also be evil as well. That's precisely why I felt the need to share what I know so far with you. Are these entities drawn to children and the young, or is it just that these are the ones who are more prone and open to being susceptible to seeing something like this? A humanoid creature so unknown and bizarre makes me wonder what else is lurking around our children that most of us can't see.

I don't know if I have ever had an encounter with one of these entities, so I also must wonder if they are new, and if so, why are they appearing all over the place now? Here are two encounters I wanted to share with the public, and hopefully you will be able to make your own assumptions and draw your own conclusions after hearing them.

Our first is from a person who gave an account of her own personal experiences with these beings from when she was younger. She was about eight years old at the time and was sitting in what she called "a lounge at the end of a hallway" in her home. She claims not to be able to clearly remember exactly what she was doing in this "lounge" but that she remembers the encounter quite vividly. She reported, "All of a sudden, I had a really powerful urge to look at the end of the hallway. We had recently brought a coat stand from a boot sale and this was in the middle of the hallway now. As I stood there I saw a human outline but entirely filled with TV like static. I remember little bits of yellow and blue in it but it was mainly white and it came out of the bedroom on the left and was in a running stance but it was really weird because it was in slow motion and it ran from the left to the back door on the right. As it ran it grabbed the coat stand and pulled it down with it and it fell to the floor. I was just standing there in shock and so scared. I ran to my sister and told her what happened and when we went back to the hallway the stand was still on the floor. That was the only time I saw it, I don't know why I saw it or why it pulled the stand down. It was all just surreal. I did have some other experiences in that house that were paranormal so maybe it was connected."

There's a similar encounter that also happens to a

little kid inside his own home. A place where he is supposed to feel safe, but I'm pretty sure after this, that security was at least somewhat shattered. He said he was getting up in the middle of the night to get a glass of water. For some reason he still can't explain, he says he went into his parents' room after getting the water. This was not normal, as he would get the water and go back to his room to go back to bed. He slept in his own room at the time and says the only thing he can think of is that he was being drawn to his parents' room for some reason.

This witness stated about his encounter, "When I walked into their room (no door) I saw on the other side of their bed a huge humanoid shape that looked like it was made of static from a TV, except the white was purple, and kind of like when you rub your eyes through your eyelids. I immediately just laid down and went to sleep right there and woke up there in the morning. Don't think I ever told anyone about it until years later. I was 3 or 4 so it's possible my imagination just went nuts but it always stuck with me."

I also came across some recurring encounters. Someone who encounters the entity first as a little kid or small child and then receives visitations or encounters the entity again, multiple times throughout their life. This next witness says that from very early on in his childhood he has had experiences where he would see "visual snow" over his regular field of vision. Kind of like that white and/or gray static that used to always be on televisions way back in the day when they would go off for the night or when the channel didn't get reception, but laying over everything he was looking at. Suddenly humanoid forms would take shape out of this... well, this visual white noise. Can we call it tangible white noise at this point? According to *Mysterious Universe*, "These entities congeal out of the static, seemingly made of this visual snow, and, according to him, appeared 'in corners, at the edge of the bed, in windowsills, and "dancing" in fields.'"

This phenomenon haunted our witness throughout his childhood, but he always thought it was just poor vision and pareidolia. However, when in later years he had corrective eye surgery done, the phenomenon did not go away, and neither did the entities. The witness says of his experiences, "I was incredibly myopic and I have an astigmatism. However, last December I had prk—a laser eye surgery, and the static never went away. Because it's always been there, if I'm not focused on it I can sort of tune out the static (like a white noise) and that's how I usually go about the day to day. When I was a kid I always told myself it was just my imagination, but laying in my bed at night it was hard to believe it was all in my head. Now, in the past four years, I've stopped trying to ignore them. I don't avidly seek them out, but I must admit that there is something magnetic about them. I'm not sure if I'm making any sense; the whole situation is difficult to describe. First, comes the anxiety. Then I see them, and then something just clicks. It could just be depersonalization or derealization, but it's all so very surreal. I try to draw features when I can, but the more I focus on them the more their features seem to shift without moving. I used to think they were aliens. I was always terrified of aliens. Then I thought they were the 'Good Folk.' Now I believe that it's all the same. To me it doesn't really matter if they're a figment of my mind, or an actual entity (aliens or fairies or ghosts or whatever). Regardless of the nature of their existence—I see them. Others see them. So something, somehow—some way, must be there."

Throughout all of the encounters I sifted through when deciding which ones to put in this book, I never came across a single encounter where these entities harmed anyone, not physically anyway. They differ from shadow entities in that right, in a way, kind of. It's more uncommon than not for a shadow entity to simply instill fear, terror and dread into its victims instead of attacking them. The encounters and witness statements vary so greatly though and there are so many labels and headings under which I put specific and certain types of shadow beings that I can't even keep up anymore. That doesn't mean I'll stop though.

Chapter 18
More Bizarre Shadow Encounters

Our first strange and terrifying encounter comes from someone whom we will call "Kyle" for the sake of his anonymity. Kyle is a nonbeliever in all things paranormal, or at least he says he was, up until this night, when he had this encounter. Now, fifteen years later, he still has no clue what happened on that dark and stormy night.

Kyle was sixteen years old and sharing a basement/recreation room with his twin brother, Jason. They both used it as a bedroom, but Kyle says his parents painstakingly built it for them, and it was separated by a door. Basically, it was made into two rooms. One night Kyle was startled awake at around three in the morning by his brother banging on the door of his room, which led into Kyle's room, which then led up the stairs and into the house proper. His brother was yelling that he was stuck in his room; he couldn't get the door unlocked and desperately needed to use the bathroom. Kyle went to jump up so he could go and help his brother with the door but found he was completely paralyzed from the neck down. Oddly enough he did have use of his head and not just his eyeballs as is usually the case. Kyle tried to scream to his brother that he was stuck and couldn't move, but no sound would come out. He lay there, terrified and listening to his brother beg him to come and help open the door, but was useless to do anything.

After what seemed like an eternity but what he now recognizes was only a minute or two, Kyle was able to move again and almost leapt out of bed to go and help his brother. Jason was pounding on the door so hard that it was actually shaking. Kyle tried turning the knob, but it wouldn't budge. Jason was right. The door seemed to be locked, but that was impossible because there was no lock on it at all. Jason was screaming, "Kyle, stop messing around and come and help me open the door!" Kyle told his brother to wait right there while he went and got a screwdriver to try to remove the doorknob for him. Kyle explained that to this day he has no idea why he did what he did next, but he thinks it is what saved his life and possibly his brother's as well. Kyle says he decided, for some unknown reason, to look through the little window on top of the door. What he saw chilled him to his bones and made him wonder if he was really awake and experiencing all of this at all or if he was stuck inside some sort of lucid nightmare.

There, on the other side of the door and speaking

clearly and concisely and sounding exactly like his brother was a dark black mass that looked to be floating about two feet off the ground and wearing a hooded cape. What really stuck out to Kyle, though, was the thing's eyes. They were glowing yellow. Kyle stared for another minute and noticed that every time this thing mimicked his brother's voice, its eyes would blink on and off from yellow to darkness, nothing. He yelled through the door to his brother to wake up, but it seemed as though Jason couldn't be woken up.

Kyle was just about to run up the stairs to get his parents, but when he turned around, his brother's door was open, and there was no sign of the creature that had just been there seconds ago. Kyle was absolutely terrified and curled up in a fetal position in his bed and didn't sleep for the rest of the night. The next morning his brother woke up and told the family about a strange and very vivid nightmare he had had the night before. He said in the nightmare Kyle had been banging on his bedroom door and screaming about needing to borrow his phone charger, but when he got up to try to open the door, it was locked. He also talked about a very tall and dark mass, floating off the floor with blinking yellow eyes, which he saw was standing over Kyle's bed and whispering in his ear. Kyle didn't say anything and kind of just went on about his life. However, once he finally started searching for evidence of what he had seen being real, he couldn't stop. It's still an obsession of Kyle's to this day though he hasn't ever seen the creature, or any other otherworldly being, ever again.

What did this thing want, and why was it trying to get each brother to the door? I don't believe for a second that either one of these young men were dreaming, and I cautioned Kyle to watch what he researches and how much, lest he fall into some sort of demonic trap or subject himself to full-blown possession.

Our next report comes from a witness who says they are absolutely sure that shadow entities are never benign and that all of them are some sort of Djinn or demon. They claim to have had many encounters and insist there is nothing good or light in these terrifying bedroom invaders.

Our witness was visiting his hometown and staying a week with his mother in the house he had grown up in. He lay in his bed and watched some television before turning it off and trying to drift off for the night. He said it was now pitch black in his bedroom, which never seemed to have bothered him before this night. He had slept in this room his entire life until he moved out and started a family of his own ten years ago. He and his children and his wife have all stayed in this room at one time or another, and that's what he said made this encounter all the more terrifying; he imagined what his children had seen and encountered.

Despite all of the windows in his room being locked up tight and both the bedroom door and the one to the closet being closed, he heard someone skulking around in his room. Our witness thought that maybe it was his mother, who was coming in to say goodnight to him again or to ask him to help her with something before she went to bed. He was a bit annoyed because he was exhausted, but he sat up and turned towards the bedroom door to see who was there. He looked just in time to see an all-black, extremely dark shadow figure standing there in front of the bedroom door. It was about seven or eight feet tall, and he explained that, despite the room being pitch black, he could see this thing very clearly. That's how dark these entities are; they are darker than the darkest darkness we know as human beings.

He somehow found his voice and demanded to know what the entity wanted from him and what it was doing in his bedroom. When he asked the questions, the figure took a step closer to him, and he realized he was now paralyzed, in a sitting position, and unable to get out of the bed or otherwise escape the grasp of this evil and malevolent creature. He knew, as most victims do, right down to the depths of his soul that this thing was pure evil. He tried to scream but couldn't, and the thing got so close to him that if it had had breath, our witness would have smelled it. The entity then seemed to be mocking him as it opened its "mouth" and seemed to be pulling something, some sort of essence, out of the victim. Within a couple of eternal seconds, the entity vanished, and the man fell back down onto his bed. He explained it was more like he was pushed down, or as he put it, "Let go. Let out of whatever grip it had on me as it sucked away my very essence; as it feasted on my fear and terror."

I always love encounters from nonbelievers and from people who feel as though they have the phenomenon pinned down. They are the ones who seem to act more boldly, like asking demanding questions and honestly expecting an answer from the beings themselves. Despite also being convinced it is a demon or the devil himself.

Our witness said he turned the TV back on and didn't sleep much for the rest of the night. He asked his mother and brother who lived in the house if they had ever had any experiences with a shadow figure, and he also asked his wife and kids. The answer was a resounding no, and he still can't explain, or forget about, what he saw and experienced that night.

Our last encounter comes from someone who has been having experiences with shadow people since they were a child. I don't find many people like me, so I thought I would share her experience here.

Tara had three imaginary friends as a kid. All three of them were shadow beings, all of different heights and sizes. There was a head and neck shape for each one, but right around where the chest areas should have been, the three figures sort of blended together to make one figure. This one figure had three different length tendrils at the end of it. Think of how cartoons show the bottoms of genies who come out of lamps, like that. That's how she knew they were three different sizes, by where these three tendrils fell. Tara remembers not being initially afraid of these beings and that she actually took them into her confidence. There were times when she would just sit in her room and converse with these strange beings. It was like she felt some kind of connection with them, as if they were supposed to be with her. These beings never communicated back with her, as far as she can remember anyway, and the visitations, which at that point were almost daily and nightly, ended when she entered the sixth grade.

Now, let's break this down. Could these beings have actually been imaginary? Could Tara's young and active imagination have made such creatures up? Sure, anything is possible. However, it's highly unlikely that she would make something up that would turn out, thirty years later, to be fast becoming a sensational and recognized phenomenon by all different types of people who are experiencing them all across the world.

In Tara's case I wonder if these particular entities had some sort of extraterrestrial origin, and perhaps they were some sort of guardians to her. Without knowing what her home and school life was like at the time she was seeing them, though, I have no way of really knowing. Sometimes when a hybrid comes to earth, they really and truly struggle. Hybrids, starseeds, earth angels, indigo children, extraterrestrials in general and even golden children such as myself, rare as we are, all have guardians assigned to us from our place of origin. It doesn't matter where the place we are from is, as the possibilities are as limitless as what the shadow beings actually are. Maybe Tara was struggling in her life and with having incarnated here on this supposed prison planet. Perhaps these entities were guides of some sort that chose to present themselves as shadows in order to protect Tara from fearing them too much. Maybe their true identities are something either our human eyes can't perceive or that our human minds cannot comprehend. Maybe they did communicate with her, either telepathically and she can't remember or subconsciously, and the information will be activated in her when the time is right. These are a lot of hypotheticals, I am aware, but that's really all we have to go on, so we may as well think big! At least that's my opinion.

Chapter 19
My Final Thoughts

As someone who has a lot of experience in dealing with all things paranormal and otherworldly, I find that shadow entities are one of, if not the most elusive of all supernatural beings. Most people want to just pretend as though there is some medical cause for it or that it didn't really happen the way they remember. The problem with that though is, if this were the case, then how is it that thousands of people the world over are all experiencing the same exact entity? In my opinion, that just isn't possible.

I think the Djinn are very real and the most evil of all. I believe the Djinn are more evil than the devil himself or any of his minions. Could they be working in tandem? It's possible. I also believe there are shadow beings who are ancient native spirits who roam the earth looking for sensitive souls to take their revenge out on.

A lot of the time the shadow entity phenomenon is generational. If your parents have had encounters with them, most likely you or one of your siblings will as well. I am currently trying to find some data on the personal traits of the people who are victimized by these shadows and see if maybe a certain nationality or religion is prone. So far, I don't have enough factual data to make even an educated guess on that, though.

As someone who has had so many beautiful, heavenly and joyful experiences with higher elevational beings of love, light and peace, I often wonder about these darker energies. Are they something that perhaps, even if unintentionally, I am bringing on myself with all of my research into the darkness?

Some of my clients are convinced the shadow entities they are seeing are the souls or energy of people they loved who have died. They wholeheartedly believe that perhaps these loved ones are unable to take on a full form and therefore have no choice but to appear in shadow. It's then that I will ask them if they get any sort of uplifting or peaceful feeling from any of their encounters. The answer is always a resounding no, and though I hate to be the one to burst their bubble, I've been dealing with all kinds of dead people, both once living and never having been human, and I know better. There is no chance, at least in my opinion, going by what I've learned through years of personal experience, dealing with clients' experiences and research into shadow entities, that these things are anything light or good. That primal feeling of terror and dread and the smell of death or sulfur that's sometimes associated with them as well lead me to believe that they are wholly and purely evil. This is a defense or survival instinct that was given to us by the Creator in order for us to be able to recognize when there is evil around us. In some cases, depending on the relationship you have with your own guides and angels, it's them putting these dreadful feelings into your body and core as a sort of warning.

Throughout centuries and since the beginning of time there have been reports of shadow beings and their attacks on not only humans in general but on their psyches as well. They seem to want to devour us. Every ounce of dread and every drop of fear and over the course of time. In most cases the encounter isn't a one-off and happens throughout a lifetime, albeit sporadically. This is why I always encourage my loved ones and clients to find something that enables them to believe in something bigger than themselves. Whether that be a Higher Power or simply their Higher Selves, it's always a good thing to commune, in whatever way you see fit, with these extradimensional and otherworldly beings who are pure light and just waiting to be invited to not only educate but to protect us as well. Pray if you believe that is where your light will come from, meditate if that's your thing, speak aloud to the Divine in your life, who or whatever it is and see how fast your life changes and how much more light will be poured into it.

As far as the shadow entities are concerned,

beware of them. They aren't going away anytime soon and, in fact, seem to be the most encountered supernatural or otherworldly entity in the twenty-first century. There is no escaping them and no knowing when they will appear and strike. They could be the monster under your bed or the creature in your closet. They could be everything you've ever feared in your entire life, and they will make your nightmares a living reality if you aren't careful.

Acknowledgments

I would like to acknowledge first and foremost God and Jesus Christ who, without them none of this would be possible. My family and close friends who are always there to support me when I'm struggling and who believed in me when I couldn't believe in myself. All of those who regularly attend my Wednesday night stream and support, encourage and believe in me on a regular basis- I appreciate and love you all so much and owe so much of my success to all of you. Steven Lee Davis (Ghostdragonzw) my best friend in the world I don't know what I would do without you, and I love you dearly. My children for putting up with me and being my biggest fans- never give up on your dreams!

About the Author

Gemma Jade was born and raised in Passaic County, New Jersey and has always felt drawn to the paranormal and supernatural world. She saw her first full bodied apparition at the age of four and was more interested in than terrified of it. Once she was old enough she started to seek answers. Gemma is of Native American and Irish descent and was fascinated by the old legends from both countries. She first encountered the fairies and their magic when she was

7 and her paternal grandmother from the Irish old country would tell her of the myths and legends of "the Little Ones." Gemma was and continues to be lured by the unknown. She is also a clairvoyant and clairsentient psychic and credits this to her native American blood. She currently resides in Morris County, New Jersey.

Gemma has taken her research and search for all things paranormal, supernatural and unexplained to her youtube channel titled simply Gemma Jade. She has joined with Steve Stockton to livestream and communicate with other like minded individuals who are searching for the truth. They talk a lot about the missing in the woods, and of course the fae. Gemma's focus on her channel is also to bring light to missing person's cases happening all over the world both inside and out of the woods. She has even given a platform to her viewers where they cannot only feel safe in telling their own encounters, but also where they can communicate with like minded individuals in her community.

Join Gemma on her channel here: https://www.youtube.com/c/GemmaJadeYT

Also by Gemma Jade

Missing: The Fae Theory

Encounters with Evil: 101 True & Terrifying
Stories

www.ingramcontent.com/pod-product-compliance
Lightning Source LLC
Chambersburg PA
CBHW032349280326
41935CB00008B/501